D0934983

The Archaeology of American Labor and Working-Class Life

The American Experience in Archaeological Perspective

UNIVERSITY PRESS OF FLORIDA

Florida A&M University, Tallahassee
Florida Atlantic University, Boca Raton
Florida Gulf Coast University, Ft. Myers
Florida International University, Miami
Florida State University, Tallahassee
New College of Florida, Sarasota
University of Central Florida, Orlando
University of Florida, Gainesville
University of North Florida, Jacksonville
University of South Florida, Tampa
University of West Florida, Pensacola

The American Experience in Archaeological Perspective
Edited by Michael S. Nassaney

The books in this series explore an event, process, setting, or institution that was significant in the formative experience of contemporary America. Each volume will frame the topic beyond an individual site and attempt to give the reader a flavor of the theoretical, methodological, and substantive issues that researchers face in their examination of that topic or theme. These books will be comprehensive overviews that will allow serious students and scholars to get a good sense of contemporary and past inquiries on a broad theme in American history and culture.

The Archaeology of American Labor and Working-Class Life

Paul A. Shackel

Foreword by Michael S. Nassaney

University Press of Florida

Gainesville/Tallahassee/Tampa/Boca Raton

Pensacola/Orlando/Miami/Jacksonville/Ft. Myers/Sarasota

Copyright 2009 by Paul A. Shackel
Printed in the United States of America. This book is printed on Glatfelter Natures
Book, a paper certified under the standards of the Forestry Stewardship Council (FSC).
It is a recycled stock that contains 30 percent post-consumer waste and is acid-free.
All rights reserved

14 13 12 11 10 09   6 5 4 3 2 1

Library of Congress Cataloging-in-Publication Data
Shackel, Paul A.
The archaeology of American labor and working-class life / Paul A. Shackel ;
foreword by Michael S. Nassaney.
p. cm.—(The American experience in archaeological perspective)
Includes bibliographical references and index.
ISBN 978-0-8130-3410-2 (alk. paper)
1. Industrial archaeology—United States. 2. Historic sites—United States.
3. Excavations (Archaeology)—United States. 4. Material culture—United States—
History. 5. Labor—United States—History. 6. Working class—United States—History.
7. Labor movement—United States—History. 8. United States—Antiquities.
9. United States—History, Local. I. Title.
T21.S53 2009
331.0973—dc22   2009019218

The University Press of Florida is the scholarly publishing agency for the State University System of Florida, comprising Florida A&M University, Florida Atlantic University, Florida Gulf Coast University, Florida International University, Florida State University, New College of Florida, University of Central Florida, University of Florida, University of North Florida, University of South Florida, and University of West Florida.

University Press of Florida
15 Northwest 15th Street
Gainesville, FL 32611-2079
http://www.upf.com

Contents

Figures

Foreword

The potential energy of America's rivers was not lost on early settlers and later industrialists as they constructed gristmills, saw mills, canals, and textile factories to enable local production and decrease dependence on overseas goods. Although the adoption of water power for industry had its origins in Europe, the technological developments associated with the industrial revolution had a dramatic impact on the American experience. Labor relations, living conditions, and landscapes throughout the nation were shaped by a capitalist mode of production. In examining American global ascendancy in the late nineteenth and twentieth centuries, historians have typically celebrated the feats of industrial giants such as the Rockefellers, J. P. Morgan, and Andrew Carnegie at the expense of telling the story of the working class. The way in which labor is portrayed in the postindustrial era is not inconsequential to how we see ourselves as a nation. Capitalism has an uncanny way of managing to cover its own tracks by muting the voices of the majority, and scholars have been complicit in this charade. For instance, the field of industrial archaeology has generally perpetuated the successes of capitalism and avoided discussion of labor and its efforts to resist conditions of inequality. Evidence of this struggle is all around us, though it is often undetected, ignored, misunderstood, or purposefully hidden.

As a child whose grandparents immigrated to the Blackstone River Valley for employment in the cloth industry, I rambled among factory ruins near the millpond in my hometown of Central Falls, Rhode Island, which takes its name from the falls immediately above those that powered the famous Slater Mill. Incorporated in the 1870s, Central Falls boasted more than twenty thousand residents in the 1920s, most crammed into tenements and boardinghouses in the square-mile city. Like many other places in the United States, Central Falls has chosen to ignore if not deliberately forget its past. Its motto—"A friendly city with a forward look"—urges visitors and newcomers to envision the future, not the past. In a place that remains dominated by the working class, there is practically no historic preservation, and even costly demolition occurs infrequently. Yet many reused buildings stand as testimony to a time when belts, pulleys, and turbines powered machines that produced fabrics and thread to clothe the world. One factory that was converted into housing for the elderly literally overlooking the falls is particularly ironic since men and women who once toiled there now live out their remaining days in the same building.

As historical archaeologists have demonstrated repeatedly, vestiges of the industrial landscape remain well preserved, waiting identification, investigation, and interpretation in many parts of the world. Moreover, careful investigation of this material record is likely to invoke experiences different from those documented in official histories. In *The Archaeology of American Labor and Working-Class Life*, Paul A. Shackel aims to center labor in the story of industrial life. He argues that American industrial capitalism—the most formative political-economic process of the past 150 years—must be examined from the perspective of labor and the working class to fully understand the American experience. Labor has often been ignored at the expense of capital and corporate success in the history of American industry. Shackel calls for greater balance by looking at that history from the point of view of labor. By doing so we are better positioned to examine the costs as well as the benefits of industrialization. This book takes the opportunity to situate the study of labor and the working class in ways that can transform industrial archaeology as it is currently practiced.

Profitability has always been central to success in the competitive arena of capitalist markets. Managers on behalf of owners enforced time discipline, reorganized space at home and in the workplace, separated the conception of the product from its execution, and created the American system of interchangeable parts to segment the labor process and deskill the work force. These technical innovations simultaneously solved the problem of the labor shortage in the nineteenth century and served to inculcate standardized models of worker behavior. These new practices were legitimized through ideologies that reinforced increasing disparities in wealth and status, as capital reproduced conditions of inequality by extracting surplus labor from workers. The practices and ideologies associated with the making of the working class were grounded in the material world.

Shackel reveals how places and objects evident in documentary sources, the archaeological record, and heritage sites can contribute to understanding the importance of industrial labor and its challenges and struggles vis-à-vis capital. Of particular interest is the materiality of labor conditions and how it can be further studied by scholars and interpreted to the public as an aspect of American heritage. Shackel surveys various archaeological studies that have documented patterns of inequality at home and in the workplace to illuminate the ways in which labor attempted to regain some degree of autonomy in a system that minimally tolerated deviation from prescribed behaviors. From discarded cutlery wasters to empty beer bottles and anachronistic ceramic sets, Shackel discusses how the archaeological record and the built environment can be understood as a product of the struggles between workers and managers. The collective response was the "hard won rights of workers to acquire better work conditions and a decent standard of living." A popular bumper sticker reminds the reader of the accomplishments of the labor movement, including the eight-hour work day and the weekend. To ignore this historical reality risks distorting the past in the interest of industrial capital. Archaeology also helps us recover *from* the past. Heritage sites need not be places to wallow in injustice but ones in which we can come to a new resolve about the past and our place in transforming the world.

In the end, we must understand industrialism to understand ourselves because issues surrounding labor intersect with social identities such as race and gender as well as the deteriorating environmental conditions that many people are compelled to live with daily. Many contemporary problems, such as pollution or the severed ties between employers and communities, have their roots in the forces that drive industry to be competitive no matter what the human costs. The strategies of multinational corporations to outsource for cheaper labor have their roots in the past, underscoring the complex relationship between past and present. A closer, multivocal reading of the past also reminds us that the conditions of labor and the working class were by no means inevitable, and careful contextual study provides potential models for alternate futures.

Michael S. Nassaney
Series Editor

Preface

In Ralph Ellison's *Invisible Man*, the protagonist reflects on how our society remembers:

> All things, it is said, are duly recorded—all things of importance, that is. But not quite, for actually it is only the known, the seen, the heard and only those events that the recorder regards as important that are put down. . . . What did they ever think of us transitory ones? We who write no novels, histories or other books. What about us? (Ellison 1952:332)

When reading this passage, I think about all the people who have been overlooked or misrepresented in the many narratives about our nation. We are good at supporting the powerful histories associated with the development of industrialization and industrial capital, and we continue to celebrate the feats of the robber barons, those businessmen and bankers in the late nineteenth and early twentieth centuries who amassed great wealth. However, we have not been good at recognizing that exploitation of the working class by the robber barons is what allowed for their vast accumulation of material wealth. Although capital and labor struggle to make their respective stories part of the national public memory, more times than not, the story of the benefits of industrialization is more prominent on the landscape than that of the hardships faced by the working class. Stories about race, gender, and class have often been downplayed or overlooked, and historical archaeology is a discipline that can help reveal some of the unmentioned, hidden, and forgotten histories.

Industrialization dramatically changed the landscape and the way most Americans live. Labor, time discipline, mass transportation, mass manufacturing, and a growing working class are all results of the new industrial culture. Between the American Civil War and World War I, a period known as the Gilded Age, industrialization shaped and significantly changed the growing U.S. economy. By the early twentieth century, the United States had been transformed from a mostly rural and agricultural society to a largely urban and industrial culture. Unchecked industrialization led to deteriorating living conditions for urban laborers and the working poor, as well as a change in working-class domestic life. As Mark Twain and Charles Dudley Warner (1972 [1873]) noted, the Gilded Age was anything but. It was a time in U.S. history characterized by ambition, in which wealth was consolidated through the operation of new technologies and novel corporations and arrangements of capital. W. E. B. Du Bois perceived the Gilded Age for what it was: To people of color and most of the rest of the country, it was a time in which industrialists dominated the transportation networks, natural resources, and economic base for much of the nation, frequently through subsidies from the federal government or with the help of purchased politicians (Du Bois 1935). The Gilded Age created new wealth for the robber barons, but the working class received few benefits for their labor. When the cycles of capital contracted during various panics, recessions, and depressions, it was often these laborers who suffered the most.

While the history of capitalism in the United States can easily provide successful examples of industrialization, a new working class developed, one that had very few rights and was at the mercy of industrialists such as Andrew Carnegie, John D. Rockefeller, and J. P. Morgan. From 1880 to 1900, about 35,000 workers died annually and another 536,000 were injured each year due to industrial accidents(Dubofsky 1996:24). In the late nineteenth century, workers who were injured on the job could be compensated for their injury only through litigation. Under common law the courts assumed that workers should understand dangerous working conditions and that they had the freedom to leave these situations and find employment elsewhere. If they stayed in dangerous jobs and were injured, the employer could not be blamed legally. Litigation was only successful if the worker could prove that the employer had directly caused the accident. Workers' compensation, which was legislated in the Progressive era, took the issue out of the courts and made immediate payment to the injured worker. Such legislation was first passed in New York state in 1910, but by the end of World War I all states had enacted workers' compensation laws (Go 1996:401–402). During the early years of industrialization, however, workers' situations were also compounded by low wages and poor living conditions.

Violent strikes occasionally erupted, pitting capital against labor. Social reformers worked for better working and living conditions and lobbied against the use of child labor. As late as 1920, factory workers labored an average of more than fifty hours per week, and steel workers labored sixty-three hours per week. Workers fought hard for the eight-hour work day, and they continually struggled for safer working conditions and a chance to have a decent standard of living (Dubofsky 1996:24).

Near the end of World War II, in January 1944, Franklin Roosevelt's proposed, in his state of the union address to Congress, a second bill of rights intended to benefit the growing working class. While many critics say the speech was far from elegant, and it has been lost in the memory of the war, it "has a strong claim to being the greatest speech of the 20th century" for what it proposed (Sunstein 2004:B9).

Roosevelt argued that while the war was winding down in Europe, the United States must invest in security, including physical security, economic security, social security, and moral security. He explained that "essential to peace is a decent standard of living for all individual men and women and children in all nations. Freedom of fear is eternally linked with freedom from want" (Sunstein 2004:B9). He later insisted, "We cannot be content, no matter how high that general standard of living may be, if some fraction of our people—whether it be one-third or one-fifth or one-tenth—is ill-fed, ill-clothed, ill-housed, and insecure" (Sunstein 2004:B9).

In his address, Roosevelt reviewed some of the important elements of the Constitution and the Bill of Rights, noting that U.S. citizens had some inalienable political rights, including freedom of speech, freedom of the press, freedom of worship, trial by jury, and freedom from unreasonable searches and seizures. However, he thought that these rights needed to be expanded. Roosevelt claimed that we had to come to a "clear realization of the fact that true individual freedom cannot exist without economic security and independence" (Sunstein 2004:B9).

He proposed that a second bill of rights be established for all—regardless of station, race, or creed. He then listed the relevant rights: (1) the right to a useful and remunerative job in the shops, farms, or mines of the nation; (2) the right to earn enough to provide adequate food and clothing and recreation; (3) the right of every farmer to raise and sell his products at a return which will give him and his family a decent living; (4) the right of every businessman, large and small, to trade in an atmosphere of freedom from unfair competition and domination by monopolies at home and abroad; (5) the right of every family to a decent home, (6) the right to adequate medical care and the opportunity to achieve and enjoy good health; (7) the right to adequate protection from the economic fears of old age, sickness, accident, and unemployment; and (8) the right to acquire a good education.

Although Franklin Roosevelt died fifteen months after delivering his address, Eleanor Roosevelt played a major role in incorporating these ideas in the United Nations' Universal Declaration of Human Rights in 1948. The ideas in the second bill of rights are today found in the constitutions of Finland, Spain, Ukraine, Romania, Syria, Bulgaria, Hungary, Russia, and Peru. Article 14 of the interim Iraqi constitution, celebrated by the George W. Bush administration, states that "the individual has the right to security, education, health care, and social security" (Sunstein 2004:B10).

Framing our work in a larger historical context is always important as we dig deeper for the meaning of domestic and industrial sites. While this book focuses on the American experience, it is always important to think about the context in which our archaeology is done and how it might be used to tell different stories that counter the dominant narrative that supports industrialist consensus histories. Henry Glassie (1977:29) describes history as the "myth[s] for the contemporary power structure." Those performing archaeology of the industrial era must also think about how their work supports these myths, or provides new and alternative views to the past. I also think it is important to keep Roosevelt's second bill of rights in mind when we think, study, and write about labor and working-class people. Roosevelt saw internal threats (such as poverty, health, and education) and external threats (such as aggression and antidemocracy movements) as reason to broaden the rights of all Americans. Many of the issues listed in the second bill of rights are important research topics that can be part of any archaeology of the industrial era. We need to make these rights part of our teaching and research agendas. I challenge all of us to think about the past in reference to these issues and see how we can change the present and think about how we can influence future.

Acknowledgments

My interest in issues related to labor and the working class came early in my life. Many of my family members were active in labor unions in the New York area. You were a success if you learned a trade and earned your union card. Some family members thought I was going to be a welder. Instead, I went to an archaeology field school and became a professor at a land-grant university (our faculty is not unionized). I can't help but think that a few of my family members may be disappointed. However, I still remember my roots and the lessons I learned about justice and the need for basic human rights for all.

During my early graduate career I made the connection between labor and archaeology after many discussions with Mark Leone, who also introduced me to the writing of Michel Foucault. My work at Harpers Ferry, West Virginia, allowed me to extend this work into the nineteenth century. While designing the project for Harpers Ferry I benefited from several discussions I had with Stephen Mrozowski. He gave me several valuable pointers and described some of the lessons learned in the project that he codirected with Mary Beaudry at Lowell. Stephen Pendery showed me around Lowell, Massachusetts; Janina O'Brien, a former resident of Lowell, provided me with a few references as well as some context related to growing up in the town; and Jane Baxter spent time showing me the Pullman district in Chicago. Terry and Claire Martin provided me with information related to Illinois' labor history, and Donald Linebaugh shared with me his experience working with the materials at the Saugus Iron Works.

I wrote part of this manuscript while an Ethel-Jane Westfeldt Bunting Fellow at the School for Advanced Research (SAR) during the summer of 2007. Marisa Deline and Adam Fracchia helped to get this text ready for production, checking references, proof reading, and formatting the final manuscript. I appreciate the love and support I received from Barbara Little while writing this manuscript, as well as her willingness to take side trips to labor sites during our family vacations. Michael Nassaney provided in-depth comments on a first draft of this manuscript. I appreciate his time and effort to helping me make this book better and more coherent. Dean Saitta and Stephen Mrozowski also provided thoughtful suggestions on making this a better book.

Introduction

The rise of industry in the United States had an impact on landscapes, labor, gender roles, and living conditions. Today, what remains of much of the United States' early industries are rusting factories, abandoned buildings, deserted mines, scarred landscapes, and decaying inner cities and towns. These are all reminders of a U.S. economy that was dominated by industrial capitalism for more than a century. Over the past several decades communities have debated how to use these abandoned industrial properties. The strategies have included redevelopment, reuse, commemoration, and elimination. In places where communities and governments have agreed that commemoration is important, struggles sometimes develop between labor and capital about which history should be remembered at these sites. Labor issues have rarely been the focus at industrial sites, and they have not been a priority with industrial archaeologists.

Industrial sites are usually examined by specialists who document features and structures such as bridges, canals, railways, factories, mills, kilns, and mines. In the United States, industrial archaeologists are working frantically to record and preserve the remains of industries before they disappear from the landscape. As inner cities redevelop, it is often easier for developers to remove old structures rather than refit them for contemporary uses. In most cases the research and documentation of these industrial ruins are void of the stories of the people who worked in them. The study of the machine usually takes precedence over the study of people involved in the industry.

There are many who have gone to great lengths to document and popularize the technological side of industrial archaeology (e.g., Hudson 1971, 1978, 1979; Weitzman 1980). Others have charted new ways to understand the development of industrial technologies (e.g., Caplinger 1997; Harshberger 2002; Kumar 1992; Miller 2003) and the practice of industrial archaeology (Gordon and Malone 1994; Kemp 1996; Palmer and Neaverson 1998). Industrial archaeology is sometimes done to supplement the historical record by providing context and exploring issues of authenticity (Council, Honerkamp, and Will 1992:3). A major part of industrial archaeology has explained phenomena related to technological development, the economy of industry, and the industrial revolution (Gordon 2001; Stratton and Trinder 2000; Trinder 1983:218–223). These are all important works that provide the backbone for the practice of industrial archaeology.

Some scholars believe that the study of industry's physical remains and landscapes is what distinguishes industrial archaeology from other disciplines (Clark 1987:169–179; Minchinton 1983:125–136). While this approach has been important to the development of industrial archaeology, it does not necessarily encourage an interdisciplinary approach where industrial history and labor history are connected and made part of the same story. In many cases labor is not mentioned or it is considered of secondary importance when discussing industrial technology and landscapes at sites (Butler 1999:19–42; Heite 1993:43–48; Howe 1994:105–113; Pletka 1993:1–35; Rynne 2006). One prominent British industrial archaeologist notes that

> patterns of government, religious allegiance, domestic and foreign policy, patterns of trade (although perhaps not of consumer spending)—are better arrived at by other means. Familiarity with, or even interest in, all aspects of working life in the industrial period is not essential for the industrial archaeologist so long as he [sic] recognizes their existence and is prepared to ask for advice from other specialists whose interest they are. (Palmer 1990:282)

This tradition of keeping industrial archaeology focused on technology is also prominent in the United States and is reflected in IA: The Journal of the Society for Industrial Archaeology. The journal's articles are mostly about industry and technology; issues related to labor, or other questions related to the social sciences, are seldom addressed.

The editors of Industrial Archaeology: Future Directions (2005), Eleanor Casella and James Symonds, are quite clear that industrial archaeology should look at the larger implications of the industrial era and start thinking about people and how they worked and lived in industrial society. I think Marilyn Palmer (2005:60) is correct when she states that because industrial archaeologists explain their evidence in terms of technology rather than social meaning, it is difficult to get the study of industry accepted as a subdiscipline in a program because of its narrow technological focus. Others in the volume also echo this concern, including David Gwyn (2005:129) and Michael Nevell (2005:177).

Following the lead of these archaeologists, it is my contention that if the study of industry is to remain a relevant field, professionals need to pay attention to the questions that count in the larger society. Some of the most important questions in our country in the early twenty-first century revolve around issues of the environment, resources, health, and the political uses of the past, or what has become known in the United States as heritage studies. If the study of industrial sites can incorporate these issues, there could be wider support for industrial archaeology in universities and in the public sphere.

A few decades ago, several historians and anthropologists made labor a significant part of their study when examining industrial contexts (Brody 1979, 1980, 1993; Gutman 1976; Montgomery 1979; Wallace 1978). Historical and anthropological perspectives on labor help to define issues related to the impact of changing technology on workers and their families. Their work shows transformations in industry affected not only work but also domestic life and health conditions. Labor historian David Brody (1989:7–18) has also encouraged scholars to look more closely at issues related to politics and power. In historical archaeology there is an increasing call for archaeologists to include labor when examining industrial sites (Shackel 2004). A. Bernard Knapp (1998:2) writes about the importance of recognizing that technology in an industrial context must also consider labor and try to understand how people could negotiate social, political, and economic relationships. This type of study allows for few generalities, since each community and region has its own distinct history. Archaeology can play a powerful role in exploring these differences while also celebrating a common labor history. Others have also made the inclusion of labor and daily life a part of their archaeology (Beaudry and Mrozowski 1989; Brashler 1991; Costello 1998; Trinder and Cox 2000; Shackel 1996, 2000a; Van Bueren 2002; Wegars 1991; Wood 2002; Workman, Salstrom, and Ross 1994).

The interest in labor history was heightened by three groundbreaking works: E. P. Thompson's (1966) *The Making of the English Working Class*, David Montgomery's (1979) *Worker's Control in America*, and Melvyn Dubofsky's (2000) *Hard Work: The Making of Labor History*. The new labor history—from the 1960s onward—focuses on the questions of class consciousness, providing a voice for the people who have been neglected, oppressed, and considered outcasts (Dubofsky 2000:21). Thompson (1966) writes that he wants to rescue the worker from the enormous condescension of prosperity.

In a similar vein, Brooke Hindle and Steven Lubar (1988) explain in *Engines of Change: The American Industrial Revolution 1790–1860* that there are costs as well as the benefits with the development of the new industrial revolution. They focus on how industrialization changed the workplace and everyday life. They caution us not to be too celebratory over industrial technological achievements. Rather, they claim, "both benefits and costs were unevenly distributed. Some entrepreneurs benefited enormously, but many more failed, indeed some failed many times. The well-to-do often became still richer. Some workers benefited from more regular and higher wages for low-skilled work. Others found their skills dropping in value, and all workers suffered from inadequate security" (Hindle and Lubar 1988:270).

The study of labor at industrial sites follows the development of other new radical traditions, such as the civil rights movement, the feminist movement and the American Indian Movement (AIM). The new labor history, with its emphasis on workers and their families, enables the search for collective action as well as agency, resistance, gender, and class. Workers are humanized, and studying them provides a more in-depth understanding of laborers' work habits, their domestic life, their interactions within the community, and their leisure activities (Laurie 1989:7; Saitta 2007; Shackel and Palus 2006).

Remembering Industrial Labor on an International Level

Industrial sites can be found on almost every continent (e.g., Childs 1998; Donnelly and Horning 2002; Schmidt 1996). The United Nations Educational, Scientific and Cultural Organization (UNESCO) states that our cultural heritage is an irreplaceable source of life and inspiration, and the organization has been instrumental in commemorating significant industrial landscapes (2007). A 1972 international treaty adopted by UNESCO members sought to encourage the identification, protection, and preservation of cultural and natural heritage around the world considered to be of outstanding value to humanity. Among the many goals of UNESCO's World Heritage mission is to protect sites, encourage the nomination of sites, and develop site management plans. The treaty helps state systems with technical and emergency assistance as well as supporting public-awareness building activities. Today there are more than eight hundred World Heritage sites, and thirty-three are related to the heritage of industry (Shackel and Palus 2006).

England, known as the cradle of the industrial revolution, has more industrial-related sites designated by UNESCO than any other country. The Derwent Valley, which includes six communities along a stretch of fifteen miles, is known as the "cradle of the new factory system." It is recognized for its well-preserved factory buildings and as the place where the installation of the Arkwright water frame helped to develop the first continuous spinning process which could be operated by machine tenders rather than skilled operators. The invention revolutionized the British economy and transformed industrial labor. From this point forward, it became the norm for factory owners to create housing for their workers and exert a form of corporate paternalism. During this era, industrialists did not create uniform preplanned villages of the sort that became common later in the nineteenth century, such as the planned town of Saltaire, England, another UNESCO World Heritage site. Sir Titus Salt founded the town in 1853 in order to provide better working and living conditions for his workers. The mills and workers' housing were built in a harmonious style of high architectural standards. Salt provided recreation opportunities as well as a library in his town, but he had strong paternalistic control over his workers (UNESCO 2007). The town's urban plan survives intact.

While the majority of UNESCO's industrial sites are in Europe, they are also found in China, India, Bolivia, Brazil, and Mexico. None have been designated in North America. Many of these sites are included on the UNESCO list because of engineering feats such as bridges, canals, irrigations systems, aqueducts, railways, mines, iron works, or resource extraction. Many include domestic housing for workers, such as the city of Potosi in Bolivia and the remarkably well-preserved example of a small-scale rural industrial settlement associated with pulp, paper, and board production at Verla Groundwood in Finland. Crespi d'Adda in Italy is an outstanding example of the nineteenth- and early-twentieth-century company towns typically built in Europe and North America by industrialists to meet the workers' needs. The city of Røros, Norway, is linked to the copper mining industry developed in the seventeenth century and operated until 1977. The city has about eighty wooden houses occupied by workers and their families that date to the seventeenth century. They provide an example of workers' life in this mining community. Most of the houses stand around courtyards, giving the town a medieval appearance (UNESCO 2007).

Remembering Industrial Labor in the United States

While there are many UNESCO industrial sites found throughout the world, none are in the United States. One place that could be a designated site is Hall's Rifle Works at the United States Armory in Harpers Ferry, West Virginia, where interchangeable parts were first perfected in the 1820s. The process became known as the American system of manufacturing, whereby standardized, identical manufacturing processes allowed for the creation of interchangeable parts. Semiskilled workers could be used to create single parts, which led to mass manufacturing and a type of assembly line. This development revolutionized the manufacturing system. Other large-scale industrial sites that could be recognized in the United States are related to mineral extraction and the construction of dams in the West. There are also places where significant labor strikes took place—such as Haymarket (1886), Lawrence (1912), and Ludlow (1913–14)—where workers struggled for better working and living conditions for laborers and their families. Planned communities developed by industrialists also remain throughout the country, and many, such as Pullman, are well preserved. These towns and cities gained international attention as industrialists tried to find a way to attract and keep a complacent work force.

An important document that provides a good outline for understanding labor's heritage is the "The Labor History Theme Study—Archaeology Component," a draft report being developed by the National Park Service (Solury 1999). This document provides a brief overview of work cultures in the United States from the colonial period until recent times. It examines the experience of workers and addresses issues such as ethnic histories, labor mobility, community studies, worker experiences, women and minority studies, and political behavior. The report provides archaeological case studies of sites that are on the National Register of Historic Places and explores issues of labor archaeology at industrial sites. Once completed, the study will help elevate the importance of labor archaeology on the national level.

In 1987 the America's Industrial Heritage Project, now called the Southwestern Pennsylvania Heritage Preservation Commission, began a long-term project inventorying surviving historic engineering works and industrial resources in the region. Both the Historic American Buildings Survey (HABS) and the Historic American Engineering Record (HAER) as well as National Park Service programs helped to document significant industrial sites in southwestern Pennsylvania. The mission of HAER is to record industrial engineering feats, and this project has also developed several important social histories of the region. However, many of these engineering studies do not go beyond particularistic and functional inquiries, a state of the field that Thomas Leary (1979) and later George Teague (1987) cautioned us about. Nevertheless, recent work, like Mark Cassell's (2005) edited volume in *Historical Archeology* places labor in the industrial landscape.

Work by Donald Hardesty (1988, 1998) has made significant contributions to understanding the process of labor, work, and industry in the mining districts in the American West. Others have documented the mining process and life in and around mining towns in other regions across the country (Emmons 1989; Francaviglia 1992; Lingenfelter 1974; Wallace 1982). There are some noteworthy museums that describe the daily lives of miners and their families, such as the Eckley Miners' Village in Pennsylvania. The village is located near Hazleton, once the center of nineteenth-century anthracite mining. In 1969, a group of businessmen organized the Anthracite Historical Site Museum, Inc., and purchased the village of Eckley, with its two hundred residents. They deeded the land over to the state in 1971 in order to create the country's only mining town museum. Today, fewer than twenty people reside in Eckley. The town has been preserved and the museum interprets the daily living experience of mining families (Figure I.1). Exhibits discuss the hardships of life in a mining community, such as impoverishment, illness, accidents, death, and labor discontent (Wesolowsky 1996). Because public interpretations about work life do not dominate discussions of America's industrial heritage, it is an important museum with frank discussions that highlight the workers' experience.

There are a few other communities that celebrate labor while muting the voice of capital. One example is the former industrial city of Lawrence, Massachusetts. The official memory of Lawrence is presented in the Lawrence Heritage State Park, situated in the midst of the city's decaying industrial core. The museum is located in a restored boardinghouse with two floors of exhibit space devoted almost entirely to labor issues and the Bread and Roses Strike of 1912. The strike, led by young women and supported by immigrants of thirty different nationalities, closed most of the Northeast's mills as workers attempted to acquire better wages and improved working conditions. After the women walked out of the mills, the owners retaliated with force, sending in strikebreakers, the state militia, and the police. After the police killed a female demonstrator, violent clashes ensued (Figure I.2). Public sympathy for the workers escalated after the police used clubs to beat women and children (Murry 1998; Weir and Hanlan 2004). The workers

Figure I.1. Remains of a domestic structure at Eckley Miners' Village, 1996. Photograph by Paul A. Shackel.

Figure I.2. The 1912 Bread and Roses Strike. The George Meany Memorial Archives, No. 1425.

Figure I.3. Statue of mill girls in Lowell, Massachusetts, commemorating the town's early industrial development, 1998. Photograph by Paul A. Shackel.

won pay increases, time-and-a-quarter pay for overtime, and a promise of no discrimination against strikers.

Today, there are mixed reactions to remembering this strike. Some citizens believe the story should be told, while others want to forget the days of exploitation (Green 2000:57–60). "How beautiful it is to sweetly forget the clubbings of 1912, the jailings of 1919, and the clubbings again of 1931," noted one former factory worker (quoted in Green 2000:60). Today, the city remembers this labor tradition through a museum that provides a memory of labor's struggle. Like many other northeastern industrial cities, Lawrence suffered as textile mills abandoned the region from the 1920s through the 1950s in search of cheaper, unorganized labor in the southern United States. These former textile centers lost significant capital. It was not until the 1970s that some northern industrial cities were able to retool and begin revitalization. Lawrence remains one of the poorest cities in Massachusetts, suffering from the loss of its major economic base, the textile mills. The city is an example of a place that remembers the struggle of labor.

Lowell embraces its industrial past. Statues have been placed around the town to celebrate the efforts of industrial workers (Figure I.3). At Lowell

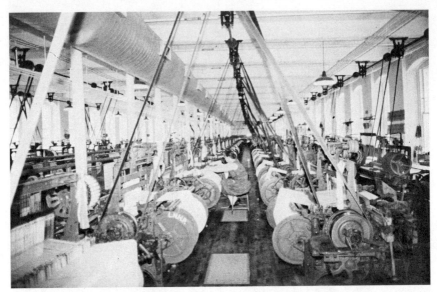

Figure I.4. Machinery operating at Lowell National Historical Park, 1998. Photograph by Paul A. Shackel.

National Historical Park, many of the exhibits present a history that includes the story of both labor and capital. For example, one exhibit extols the material benefits of industry but also explains labor strife. Visitors are also invited to walk through the mill with earplugs while more than one hundred machines operate simultaneously (Figure I.4). The experience is enough to make one realize the mental and physical strain on the mill girls and later immigrants as they labored ten hours per day.

The Museum of Work and Culture in Woonsocket, Rhode Island, interprets the experience of the French Canadian immigrant workers by using oral histories and material culture. As you venture through the exhibits you can read about and listen to the workers' stories and learn about how they coped with substandard working and living conditions. This museum exhibition effectively discusses the historical development of labor and class and shows the impact of industrialization on work, domestic life-styles, and health conditions.

The Ludlow Massacre site in southern Colorado is another place where the memory of labor dominates the landscape. While coal miners went on strike 1913 they settled in a campsite that was eventually attacked by the Colorado National Guard. Twenty people, including women and children, were killed. Today, a statue erected by the United Mine Workers of America, which depicts a miner, a woman, and a child, stands at the massacre site. The preservation of the "Death Pit" serves as a reminder of the tragedy and the site serves as a rallying point for contemporary labor struggles as people remember the tragedy at Ludlow.

The above sites are examples of how some stories of labor are represented on the American landscape and made part of the national public memory. In those rare instances when the social history of labor is communicated to the public, it is often inspired by desires of local interests. Community and labor organizations and local governments help support the stories of labor in various places across the United States.

Some Thoughts

Archaeologists have taken many different approaches to examine the relationship between labor and capital (Beaudry and Mrozowski 1989; Casella and Symonds 2005; Delle 1998; Johnson 1996; Leone 1988, 1995; Leone and Potter 1999; Little 1994; McGuire 1988; Paynter and McGuire 1991; Mrozowski 2000, 2006; Mrozowski, Zeising, and Beaudry 1996; Mullins 1996; Paynter 1988, 2000a, 2000b; Saitta 2007; Shackel 1993, 1996, 2000b, 2004; Wurst and McGuire 1999). While England is credited with the advent of the industrial revolution, by the end of the nineteenth century the robber barons of the United States controlled the world economy (Zinn 2003). The study of America's past industrial prowess tends to dominate the interpretation of industrial sites while archaeologists often overlook issues related to labor. Stephen Silliman (2006) provides an excellent, broad overview of how archaeologists treat labor studies. He notes that a focus on labor allows for the archaeologist to humanize their subjects and permits them to deal with labor sites as places of struggle (McGuire and Reckner 2002; Shackel 2004). The attention on labor helps us understand how administrators, overseers, capitalists, managers, and supervisors structured labor (Silliman 2001, 2004). While the new school of social history developed in the 1960s and called for a history from the bottom up and the inclusion of all peoples in that history, labor is often missing in our interpretations of industry. Yet it can become part of the national story.

In this book, chapter 1 presents a framework for the debate on nature of capitalism. While some scholars see capitalism as the triumph of commercial transactions over paternalistic social connections, others see the development of capitalism as the development of a new relationship between workers and capitalists. The first half of this chapter provides an overview of the large-scale contextual work developed by Eric Wolf, Immanuel Wallerstein, and Fernand Braudel, describes the development of the market system, and highlights the Europeans' search for wealth. Several archaeological studies are referenced as examples that show the development of colonization and the beginnings of modernity. The development of industrial capitalism in the United States occurred with the aid of government support for infrastructure and laws to protect capitalist ventures, the development of a new work ethic, and the creation of a new ethos to consume.

While industrialist increasingly controlled the workers through wages, they also developed new landscapes that allowed them to monitor workers in the industrial complex as well as in the domestic sphere. Chapter 2 explores these issues in well-studied landscapes, such as Lowell, Massachusetts; Harpers Ferry, West Virginia; and Binghamton, New York.

Chapter 3 examines how power is created and used in an industrial society. It describes how workers are often exploited and earn barely enough to exist from day to day. In some instances, workers resist these inhumane situations by striking, slowing down work, and committing acts of sabotage to gain some control of their situation in the workplace. Workers and their families may also purchase and use material culture in unexpected ways in order to show their resistance to the perceived dominant meaning of material goods. In other cases, charismatic leaders developed communities that were more egalitarian than what was found elsewhere in the new industrial world.

Industrialists also found ways to control the work force by supplying workers and their families with housing. Chapter 4 describes the conditions of late-nineteenth-century boardinghouses and tenement living and interprets some of the assemblages that remain in these places. The abundance of glass and other types of material culture found at these places has typically been interpreted as indicating poor sanitation practices. Using historical and ethnographic accounts of turn-of-the-century urban places provides different perspectives about health, living conditions, and strategies to make-do.

In order for an archaeology of industry sites to be viable and relevant in our society, it is important that our archaeology ask questions that count; in other words, we should ask questions that are important to society as a whole. While this book has already touched upon topics of housing and the built environment, chapter 5 shows that it also is necessary to consider the relationship between industry and gender, race, and the environment. Archaeology provides excellent examples related to issues of sustainability.

In the past, industrial development affected the environment as well as individuals and the existence of communities. These scenarios are lessons for how industrial society today threatens the ecology and human survival.

Presenting an examination of postindustrial society, chapter 6 outlines the importance of ruins and the commemoration of the industrial past. While many industrial archaeologists see that is it important to document and preserve our industrial past, some of those who labored in these factories have a very different view of what should be remembered of their working lives. Remembering labor has also not been widely accepted in different communities throughout the United States.

This book's conclusion connects many of the issues in this study to the present day. In the United States poor working conditions still exist. The U.S. Department of the State reports that at present, sweatshops employ about 100,000 to 150,000 people who are working against their will. It is important that we make these stories of labor in the past and present public, that we keep them relevant and visible by striving to address the questions that count.

1

World Systems and the Development of Industrial Capitalism

The American experience was significantly influenced by the development of capitalism because this new economic system affected landscapes, labor relations, gender roles, and general living conditions throughout the country. However, there are many competing definitions of capitalism and many ways to define its relationship to the industrial world. While different views exist, much of the scholarship on capitalism can be placed into two camps. One group sees the system as the triumph of commercial transactions over paternalistic social connections and sentimental attachment. They believe that capitalism is extensive and should be understood in a global context. Capitalism, they assert, began with the development of the modern world. A natural extension of this argument is that the early settlers of this continent were already capitalists when they arrived. On the other hand, others associate capitalism with values rooted in individualism, competition, and the development of a new relationship between worker and capitalist. The worker sells his or her labor for a wage, while the capitalist invests in machinery, pays a wage, and sells the product of the worker (hopefully for a profit) (Braudel 1979a, 1979b, 1979c; Clark 1996; Gilje 1996; Innes 1995; Kulikoff 1989, 1992; Leone 1988; Merrill 1995; Orser 1996; Wolf 1982).

While Braudel's three volumes on *Civilization and Capitalism* (1979a, 1979b, 1979c) are important for understanding the development of the modern state and the development of mercantile capitalism, I find Wolf's *Europe and the People without History* (1982) useful for providing a context for explaining the genesis of capitalism and industry in Western culture. His work, while void of archaeology, has influenced the thinking of many historical archaeologists, including my own. Wolf sees the rise of world capitalism rooted in late medieval Europe. He observes that when medieval Europeans harnessed wind and water-power technology it enabled the production of increased surplus. New technology allowed tribute-taking overlords to enhance a military class and move toward political consolidation by creating a central kingship. However, by A.D. 1300 there was a crisis in European feudalism. Available technology had reached its limits, the climate had worsened, making for an uncertain food supply, and major epidemics were killing a large portion of the population. Increased surplus became necessary to pay for war and expansion, but peasants resisted working harder and rebelled (Wolf 1982:108). Locating new resources, often in other regions, helped to solve the crisis.

The search for wealth grew dramatically, and this expansion became too large for single merchants to handle. An overarching organization, the modern state, developed, comprised of a political coalition between the centralizing executive, a class of military overlords, and the merchant class. The state protected the merchant, while the merchant lent money to the crown, paid money to the crown, and sold goods abroad. Major states that expanded overseas starting in the fifteenth century included Portugal, Spain, the Netherlands, France, and England (Wolf 1982:109–110).

World System and the Search for Wealth

Wallerstein (1976, 1980, 1989) describes the search for profit by nonproducing entrepreneurs who focused on the process of the transfer of surplus rather than the mode of production. Wallerstein shows the global connections created in order for merchants to extract surplus. An international division of labor was created by European expansion and exploitation of the periphery to the benefit of the core states (Crowell 1997:5). World systems theory is a way of explaining how lives have been affected by large-scales structures, stressing functional interactions (McGuire 2002:136). In the modern world surplus takers are seen as capitalists and the way labor is deployed is of secondary importance. The theory does not take into account the complexity of the varying modes of production that exist simultaneously. For this world systems view, "the whole world and all its parts have become similarly capitalist since that time" (Wolf 1982:297). People are caught up in historical processes beyond their control.

Since the 1980s historical archaeologists have used Wallerstein's world systems approach by developing a core-periphery model to examine the capitalist market and the world system. The core-periphery model is based on economic (and social/political) domination of outlying areas by central places. The power of the core(s) lies in its ability to control transportation and the centralization of resources and by that gain access to resources that are greater and more efficient than that of the peripheries. However, the world systems model focuses on the development of core areas and does not provide adequate attention to the development of peripheries (McGuire 2002:136–137).

Many archaeologies of the preindustrial era in the United States explore communities in the periphery and account for how they became important to core areas. For instance, the search for new wealth in the present-day United States began with the Spanish desire to control the transatlantic trade. Juan Ponce de León made an initial foray into Florida in 1513, and in the Southwest, Francisco Vázquez de Coronado's 1540–42 expedition searched for the Seven Golden Cities. In 1565 the Spanish destroyed the French-held Fort Caroline (near present-day Jacksonville) for control over La Florida. They eventually developed a system of missions along the East Coast, from Florida to as far north as a short-lived mission in the Chesapeake Bay region. These settlements established Spain's claims in the New World and provided additional protection for their fleets as they left the Caribbean laden with gold and silver for Spain.

The search for wealth in the New World and the early attempt to establish industry is noticeable from the sixteenth-century archaeological record at Roanoke. The English established the colony on Roanoke Island in 1585 when Sir Walter Raleigh and Queen Elizabeth I funded the expedition. Creating English settlements north of the Spanish stronghold in La Florida was a strategic move to subvert Spain's influence in the New World. Roanoke Island (in present-day North Carolina) is a quiet vacation area today, but for several years after 1585 it was the hope for English colonization and a potential for a new source of wealth (Quinn 1985). The island, situated behind a barrier reef off the Outer Banks, was slightly out of Spanish detection. The location could serve as a base for English privateers who could resupply their ships and harass the Spanish fleets (Quinn 1985).

The colonists built temporary dwellings and a fort, although they were more interested in searching for mineral wealth than in creating a permanent settlement. They quickly grew disheartened by the lack of precious metals and the lack of supplies from England. Archaeology conducted under the direction of pioneering National Park Service archaeologist J. C. Harrington in search of the earliest English settlement began in 1947, and similar work has more recently been led by Ivor Noël Hume. The archaeology indicates that metallurgical work occurred in Roanoke. Archaeologists uncovered a single balance weight and tiny fragments of a crucible, suggesting that experiments with metals occurred. Copper fragments show preliminary signs of smelting, probably by the expedition's metallurgist, Jochim

Ganz. It appears that he had a furnace that could reach 2,000 degrees Fahrenheit, adequate to smelt copper (Harrington 1962, 1966, 1984; Noël Hume 1983; Quinn 1985).

Archaeologists have also used the core-periphery model to explain inequalities in the archaeological record. For example, Paynter (1982, 1985) uses the model in the Connecticut River Valley to trace its change from periphery in the British system to core of its own national system. Industrialization of the region was one major factor in this transformation. The regional elite established and maintained social inequality by controlling the flow of goods and establishing entrepôts. While urban centers developed, the control of space and the flow of goods eventually led to greater disparity in wealth in the region. Pamela Cressey et al. (1982) apply this model in a citywide context using Alexandria, Virginia. Their study examines the different and changing relationships between core and peripheral economic and social areas within the city. There are ethnic and class dimensions to their work as well, since many of the oppositions are between white and black as well as between rich and poor (Cressey et al. 1982; Shephard 1987). Kenneth Lewis (1984) examines the spread of English material culture on the South Carolina frontier, and Jack Williams (1992) observes the Spanish imports and Mexican products in the northern presidios of New Spain. Aron Crowell (1997) studies the Russian occupation of Three Saints Harbor in Alaska using a world systems approach while incorporating Wolf's (1982) ideas of capitalism's impact on the world. Crowell's study examines boundary maintenance on the colonial frontier.

Charles E. Orser Jr. (1994:5) insists that historical archaeologists must look at global issues and questions that go beyond the site and community levels. Understanding the modern world and framing these studies in the broadest terms, he states, is necessary to knowing the history and development of the site. He uses the seventeenth-century maroon settlement of Palmares in northeastern Brazil as an example. Orser argues that knowing the formation of Palmares in relationship to global issues is important for understanding its connection to mercantile capitalism. Portuguese sugar plantations, Dutch settlements, Native American villages, and African communities in Angola all influenced the community's development. Orser (1996) also examines the archaeological context of Palmares and Gorttoose, a small Irish community that existed from 1780 to 1847. These two very diverse communities are connected by larger issues—colonialism, Eurocentrism, capitalism, and modernity—global forces that shaped the modern world. A global perspective that looks at the interconnectedness of the world allows for the development of a historical archaeology of the modern world. Many other works examine the development of the modern world, the exploration for resources, and the extent of interaction between groups. For instance, these works include the Russian influence on the West Coast (e.g., Lightfoot 1995; Lightfoot, Wake, and Schiff 1993; Mills and Martinez 1997), Asians working in mining camps and living urban contexts on the West Coast (e.g., Praetzellis, Praetzellis, and Brown 1987; Costello and Maniery 1988; Voss 2005), Native Americans and the process of creolization (e.g., Deetz 1963; Fitzhugh 1985), Hispanics and their search for wealth in the American Southeast and Southwest (e.g., Deagan 1983, 1987; Thomas 1989, 1990, 1991), Anglos and how their world view shaped their material surroundings (e.g., Deetz 1996), the Dutch and their search for material wealth (e.g., Huey 1991), and African Americans and their forced labor as well as their persistence in maintaining cultural traits from their native lands (e.g., Deagan and MacMahon 1995; Ferguson 1992; Orser 1988).

The world capitalist market system had an impact on gender and ethnic relations. For instance, James Deetz's (1963) pioneering study of the Chumash at La Purisima Mission in California explains the change in domestic artifacts as reflecting a form of acculturation and gender roles. He observes that native gender roles were differentially affected by the Spanish presence. His work helps to explain how the Spanish presence affected the division of labor and the nature of intercultural contact on the West Coast. David Burley's (1989) examination of material culture among the Métis is about the globalization of European material culture and how the Métis women of western Canada used European goods in gender relations. European material culture became important when white women became competitors for social positions as wives to Hudson Bay Company men. He concludes that the use of European ceramics by Métis women made them gentile and therefore legitimate wives for Euro-American men involved in the western Canadian fur trade.

Kathleen Deagan's (1973, 1978, 1983, 1985) work at St. Augustine, Florida, is important because it examines ethnic relationships and gender roles in the context of the search for wealth on a global scale. She found that Spanish ethnicity among high-status groups, such as the Spanish born *peninsulares*, is most visible in the public areas. Places that contained lower status groups, such as *criollos* and *mestizos*, tend to have a mix of Spanish and other European artifacts. In eighteenth-century St. Augustine, Deagan (1983) discovered that American Indian women in Spanish *mestizo* households primarily affected acculturation rates. Male-associated activities did not change, but wives in these households acted as cultural brokers. Others, such as David Thomas (1989, 1990, 1991) and Stanley South (1988), also have made significant contributions to understanding the creolization process in the United States.

While the above list is far from complete, much of the historical archaeology scholarship, when placed in global terms, demonstrates that European exploration and search for wealth had a far-ranging impact on people, culture, and resources. Archaeology can focus on communities and people on the periphery in order to tell a more inclusive history of mercantile capitalism and show how the search for wealth led to a globalization of material culture and influenced gender, ethnic, and class relations.

The Putting-Out System to Industrial Capitalism

Due to the development of new markets and the increased demand and flow of commodities, merchants in core areas mobilized artisans and cottage producers to develop the putting-out system. Artisans and laborers were rarely under the supervision of the owners. The risk of production and the cost of goods and production were in the artisans' hands (Wolf 1982:265). Expanding the scale and scope of operations was not completely successful, and this limited the accumulation of capital. Workers supplemented their farm work by producing products for capitalists, and they worked at their own pace. Owners often became upset because farm work, family and religious events, and entertainment could all take precedence over the supplemental work for them (Wolf 1982:274–75).

Thompson (1967:60) describes this notion of work in a task-oriented society that fostered the putting-out system, noting that guided by the cycles of nature, people's daily routines began when the sun rose and ended when the sun set. Task orientation meant the laborer focused his or her energies upon what was necessary. As a result, little demarcation existed between work life and social life, and the work day expanded or contracted according to the nature of the task. The merchant had little control over the quality and quantity of production in the putting-out system (Wolf 1982:274–275). An example of task-oriented labor comes from the diary of a small-scale farmer/weaver in eighteenth-century England. Thompson (1967:71) notes, "On a rainy day he might weave 8½ or 9 yards; on October 14th he carried his finished pieces, and so wove only 4¾ yards; on the 23rd he 'worked out till 3 o'clock, wove two yards before sunset, clouted [mended] my coat in the evening.' . . . On December 24th wove 2 yards before 11 o'clock."

Task orientation gradually shifted to a more labor oriented, standardized, and regimented society with the development of time discipline. In particular, public clocks helped regulate and standardize public life. Thompson provides an example from Workingham, England. In 1664, a sexton rang the great bell twice a day for half an hour—once at eight o'clock at night and once at four o'clock in the morning from September 10 to March 11. The bell ringing occurred so that those who "might live within the sound might thereby induce to a timely going to rest in the evening, and early arising in the morning to the labors and duties of their several callings, things ordinarily attended and rewarded with thrift and proficiency" (Thompson 1967:63).

Michel Foucault notes that disciplined behavior purports to make the best use of time and the correct use of the body: "Nothing is to remain idle . . . everything must be called upon to form the support of the act required" (Foucault 1979:152). Discipline constitutes a type of law levied onto societies, groups, and the individual. Its function is to train through repeated performance. Behavior repeated several times becomes mechanical yet fluid and natural, and it allows for an increase in efficiency of behavior (Foucault 1979:170, 177, 212). The perception of time changed along with the definition of work. Clocks replaced the rhythms of nature. Not only did public life become scheduled and routinized, but so did house life, social life, and the manufacturing process.

The eventual development of time discipline and the creation of new wealth in the Americas as well as many other factors were instrumental in creating a new economic system. Paul Gilje (1996:162–170) outlines other social, cultural, political, and economic changes necessary for the growth of industrial capitalism in the United States. He notes that first comes the development of a fluid, expansive, and extensive monetary system. Second, banks became an important vehicle for creating capital. In the 1780s and 1790s only a few banks existed, but by the 1830s more than two thousand banks had been established across the United States. While each bank printed its own notes, creating confusion and encouraging counterfeiting, the process increased the levels of capital for investment. Banks often printed more currency than what they had on hand to back the paper, but this new money aided in investments in land, transportation, industrial production, and mercantile activities. When the inflationary bubble burst, the cycle would pick up again as banks continued to support capital investment (Gilje 1996:162–164; Lamoreaux 1994).

The third change was that the emergence of the corporation became an important vehicle for capital investment. Corporation status bestowed limited liability protection. Initially, the status was given to those who pursued an activity for the general welfare of the United States, but by the mid-nineteenth century the concept of limited liability was transferred to all corporations. Corporation status encouraged risk capital or the speculation and investment in new ventures (Dalzell 1987; Hartog 1983). Fourth, encouraged investment led to the development of rapid transportation. The United States saw the turnpike boom (1790s to the early 1800s), the canal boom (1820s and 1830s), and the railroad boom (1840s and 1850s), and each new transportation network allowed for the spread of consumer goods and ideas (Taylor 1951; Brown 1989).

Fifth, the expansion of the frontier became important for the national development of capitalism. More than the westward migration of people, it became a process of speculation and investment. Fortunes were made by some, while other lost all they had. Banks funded much of this land speculation and extended money for equipment and other improvements (Hammond 1957:279–85, 622–30). Sixth came the change in the mode of production. This transformation occurred at a different rate, according to the products and technology available to the manufacturer. Usually, half-skilled laborers, who were themselves later replaced by unskilled wage laborers, replaced artisans. Workers no longer had control of the means of production (Laurie 1989; Ross 1985; Zonderman 1992).

The seventh change was that consumerism helped fuel capitalism. Scholars have debated among themselves whether production led to consumerism or if the desire for goods spurred the growth of consumerism and production (Bushman 1992; McCracken 1988; McKendrick, Brewer, and Plumb 1982; Miller 1987; Mukerji 1983). Whatever the cause, Americans sought greater material wealth through the eighteenth and into the twentieth centuries. The creation of a desire for mass-produced goods sparked a development in industrial production, from eighteenth-century Wedgewood plates to mid-nineteenth-century Singer sewing machines.

Eighth, and probably most important, is the change in the mindset, or *mentalité*, of the American public. In the eighteenth century, Americans clung to a classical republican ideology that emphasized family and community. Classical republicanism critiqued the spread of eighteenth-century consumerism in America, a criticism became popular among colonial Americans as they resisted imperial regulations and many forms of consumerism (Gilje 1996:172–173). Most American workers subscribed to a classical republican ideology; they saw themselves as citizens who could participate in the daily affairs of their community. They believed that government would act as an arbitrator between labor and capital and correct any inequalities (Ross 1985:xix). However, liberal republicanism, with its underlying concept reinforced in the U.S. Constitution, allowed the individual to act as an independent citizen, a necessary ingredient in an industrial capitalist society. By the 1820s and 1830s the pursuit of romantic ideals encouraged consumerism and the development of capitalism as liberal republicanism won out and became part of the dominant American ideology (Campbell 1987). The change occurred in the midst of a struggle between competing ideologies.

From Poor Houses to Mill Lords

Initially it was difficult attracting a labor force to the developing factory system whereby workers were centralized underneath one roof. Complying with the factory system meant conforming to a new discipline that did not fit in with the mores and customs of autonomous labor found in classical republicanism. In England, many early factories were modeled on the penal workhouses and prisons and were operated by involuntary pauper apprentices. The association of the capitalist factory with paupers and criminals was seen as demeaning to those artisans who functioned in the putting-out system.

Philadelphia modeled its early industry after the English penal workhouses, which were based on city ordinances for the unemployable poor. Both men and women were sent to city workhouses and were trained by merchants according to the regimented industrial habits of society. In the 1780s the Philadelphia prison system became synonymous with work reform and a daily schedule (Alexander 1980; Cotter et al. 1988:15–20; Cotter, Roberts, and Parrington 1992; DeCunzo 1995:14). According to Foucault (1979:125), who studied the Walnut Street Prison in Philadelphia in detail, the system helped to create the individual, an alienated laborer who operated as a replaceable worker within a larger manufacturing system. This philosophy, that prisons can be used for moral and social reform, became popular in the early nineteenth century (Casella 2001, 2007; Garman 2005). The prison, like the school, and the work place, encouraged the development of the individual under conditions of surveillance, a necessary component for the development of industrial labor.

"Houses of industry" could be found in the larger colonial cities employing poor families at spinning. This new work order helped with the cloth shortage in the colonies, and many thought it taught good habits among the poor. Workers used traditional hand-powered spinning wheels and looms in one building, where they could be closely supervised. However, a division of labor and interchangeable machinery and products did not develop for awhile (Gordon and Malone 1994). It was difficult for industrialists to recruit workers in the developing textile industry. The technological development significantly lagged behind England, which dominated the world in manufacturing textiles. England also passed laws that forbid the export of technology, and those who knew this technology were restricted from traveling abroad (Hindle and Lubar 1988:187).

In 1775 the first large-scale textile operations developed in Philadelphia. The United Company for Promoting American Manufactures employed four hundred women as spinners, most working in their own homes. The British occupation of Philadelphia brought an end to this enterprise, but after the Revolutionary War private investors and the state of Pennsylvania developed the Pennsylvania Society for the Encouragement of Manufactures and Useful Arts and reestablished the mills. The society offered a gold medal for any inventor who could create a workable power loom. It was unsuccessful in acquiring water-powered machinery and the building that housed the workers burned in 1790, three years after it was established. Unhappy handloom weavers were suspected in this case of arson (Hindle and Lubar 1988:187). Industrialists insisted that manufacturing was necessary for the new Republic's independence from European manufactured goods. The survival and security of the country depended upon the prosperity of manufacturers (Prude 1983:61; Smith 1991:4).

Samuel Slater, who served as an overseer in a British textile mill, passed as a farmer as he immigrated to America. He was then enticed by American bounties to develop technologies. Slater committed industrial technologies to memory, and in December 1790 he successfully developed a carding machine and a spinning frame powered by water. By 1793 his mill in Pawtucket, Rhode Island, became fully functional (Gordon and Malone 1994) (Figure 1.1). The mill contained the Arkwright water frame, powered by water wheels, and his work force employed nine children from the ages of seven to twelve. Slater was the first American to successfully produce cotton yarn with water-powered machines. However, since the yarn was distributed to households and families, the tradition of weaving in the home continued. The Rhode Island system, based on Slater's development and concept for manufacturing, consisted of small rural spinning mills which employed families. Slater created a system of tenant farms around his mills,

Figure 1.1. Slater Mill, Pawtucket, Rhode Island. Library of Congress, HAER, RI 4-Pawt, 3–15.

and entire families could be employed in or around the factory. This notion quickly spread through the Northeast and the middle Atlantic region and dominated advanced manufacturing through the early nineteenth century (Hindle and Lubar 1988:192). Families or an unincorporated partnership of merchants and mechanics usually owned and operated these small rural factories (Candee 1992:111).

The development of the factory system meant that large numbers of people collected under one roof and workers possessed different skills. This phenomenon was not new to the manufacturing process. What was innovative in the factory system was the new coordination of work under a unified technical management that divided labor and enforced time discipline. Dividing labor and enforcing time discipline allowed for more objects to be produced in a predetermined amount of time, and standardizing the labor process meant that anyone could perform the task. This new system synchronized the production process and created cheaper labor that could respond to the changes in market conditions (Ollman 1993:15).

A notable anthropological investigation of the early industry era is Anthony F. C. Wallace's (1978) study of Rockdale, Pennsylvania. Rockdale developed as a small cotton factory town in antebellum rural Pennsylvania. Mill owners ran the town and presided over the labor and daily affairs of the workers. The "mill lord" operated a paternalistic system and controlled the town's access to sources of money and material goods. Mill owners assumed that their power gave them the right to act as God's steward on earth (Wallace 1978:21).

The entrepreneur's responsibility included housing, feeding, clothing, and educating his employees and their families. It was also the "mill lord's" duty to train workers to be industrious and productive servants in the eyes of God. Wallace argues that while the new Republic embraced the Enlightenment ideals of progressive improvement without divine intervention, such was not true for early industrial development. Most workers became subsumed by an entrepreneurial oligarchy who acted on behalf of the divine and subjected workers to new industrial work behaviors and the disciplining and repetitive motions of the new technology and machinery (Wallace 1978:246). One mill operative, writing about her experience in Lowell, noted, "We learned no theories about 'the dignity of labor,' but we were taught to work almost as if it were a religion; to keep at work, expecting nothing else" (Larcom 1890:9).

Wolf (1982:78) describes this new capitalist mode of production as having three major characteristics. First, capitalists retain control of the means of production. Second, laborers are denied independent access to means of production and must sell their labor power to the capitalists. And third, the maximization of surplus produced by the laborers with the means of production owned by the capitalist entails ceaseless accumulation accompanied by changes in methods of production. Under the factory system, therefore, a new relationship develops between the capitalist and the worker. Governed by this new circumstance, the worker sells his or her labor to make a product, which in turn allows the capitalist to sell the item and make a profit. The worker is only being partially compensated for his or her labor, while the capitalist, who makes the initial investment in machinery and the purchase of labor, makes any profits above expenses.

While the debate between the classical and liberal republicanism continued into the early nineteenth century, liberal republicanism eventually won (Gilje 1996:172–173). An ideology developed in which all believed that the buying and the selling were a symmetrical exchange, when in fact an asymmetrical relationship developed. In reality, the laborer received part of the value of the product that they created, and the capitalist class obtained the remainder of the surplus (Wolf 1982:355). By the mid-nineteenth century the new ideology had convinced the working class that wage labor was the free choice of workers.

Some Thoughts

Defining capitalism has often been a contentious issue among scholars. Some believe that capitalism began with the development of the modern state with the expansion of mercantile capitalism. Others believe that capitalism should be defined as a new relationship between workers and capitalist whereby the worker sells his or her labor for a wage. While this book focuses on issues related to the latter concept, there is no doubt that several hundred years ago life, culture, and social relations changed as new industries created a new material wealth and changed everyday life. The material residue that resulted from these changing relationships provides an exciting avenue to explore in the archaeological record.

2

Surveillance Technologies and Building the Industrial Environment

In Foucault's view, the Enlightenment was not simply a humanitarian movement; it also created a new system of domination expressed in new surveillance technology (Foucault 1979, 1986:22–23; Tilley 1990:309). Controlling and structuring space allowed for the enforcement of a new disciplined behavior. During the Enlightenment the workplace became separated from the home and supervisors increasingly monitored workers. Tilley (1990:317) notes that the "factory-based labor process renders bodily behavior routine, repetitive, subject to codifiable rules and accessible to surveillance and calculation." The body is directly involved in a political field and "power relations have an immediate hold over it; they invest it, mark it, train it, torture it, force it to carry out tasks, to perform ceremonies, to emit signs" (Foucault 1979:22–26). The power of discipline is not that it crushes or alienates people but that it produces subjects who willingly work within the capitalist system.

Pierre Bourdieu (1977) and Foucault (1979) have observed power and discipline on the individual, group, and institutional levels. Individuals generate power, and that power in turn is supported and reinforced by other individuals and groups. It is this power which makes industrial capitalism a meta-institution supported by schools, factories, and other institutions. Discipline became successful as people were increasingly trained and monitored through surveillance, either by institutions or by peer groups. Surveillance is only successful on the level of everyday intercourse if the appropriate players understand material goods and codes of meaning.

Some of the most influential work in historical archaeology that examines the relationship between the individual and surveillance technologies in the developing modern world comes from studies in Annapolis, Maryland. Using Foucault (1979), Mark Leone (1995) and Leone and Barbara Little (1993) explain that artifacts aided in creating a self-disciplined individual, the foundation for the development of capitalism. Leone (1995:257) writes,

> Foucault explained that the imagination of the eighteenth- and nine-teenth-century citizen is an obligation to watch and also feel watched, to monitor and be monitored, to safeguard and be safeguarded, to care and be cared for. Only people who see themselves as individuals can imagine themselves this way. The notion of the individual is thus fundamental both to baroque and panoptic building plans.

The construction of the State House dome in Annapolis after the Revolutionary War was a response to the development of individualism, which was associated with liberal republicanism. The dome was intended as a surveillance mechanism "to see everyone and everything in every place and through all time" (Leone and Little 1993:162). Its design was based on Jeremy Bentham's model prison, in which all inmates could be viewed from one central position. The individual, who made up the foundation of the new government, acted in an atmosphere of the self-watching and self-disciplined citizen. It was an illusionary basis for authority and power that created hierarchy and the individual necessary for the development of industrial capitalism (Leone 1995:255).

The Nineteenth-Century Industrial Landscape

Surveillance technologies were important for the development of a controlled and disciplined work force as new urban centers developed throughout New England and the middle Atlantic region. When Francis Cabot Lowell's invention of the power loom allowed for the wholesale manufacture of cloth, he, along with fellow Bostonians, established the Boston Manufacturing Company and developed one of the first mill complexes in the United States in Waltham, Massachusetts, in 1814. Almost immediately, the Waltham mill became a great success because of its manufacturing efficiency—all of the steps of manufacturing were placed under one roof. Other industrialists saw this industrial complex flourishing, and through the 1820s and 1830s capitalists duplicated the mill's plan, which became known as the Waltham system. Their industrial factory buildings tended to have similar archaeological features, including five stories, a central tower, and brick construction. Immigrant labor helped build these new manufacturing towns. Harriet Robinson, a mill operative in Lowell, called the laborers, who were largely Irish immigrants, the "Lords of spade and shovel." In

Figure 2.1. Early-twentieth-century bird's eye view of mills in Lowell, Massachusetts. Library of Congress, USZ-62-90893.

language typical of the derogatory tone of the era, in a society that viewed the Irish at the bottom of the social hierarchy, she explained that they lived in shanties with their wives and "numerous children" in housing around the Catholic Church and, according to Robinson, spent their evenings brawling (Robinson 1976 [1898]:15–16).

The Boston Manufacturing Company, which was later renamed the Boston Associates, accumulated tremendous profits in a short time and developed other industrial centers in Lowell, Chicopee, Manchester, and Lawrence. By 1850 the Boston Associates controlled about one-fifth of the cotton production in America (Gordon and Malone 1994:96–100; Mrozowski 2006; Mrozowski, Zeising, and Beaudry 1996) (Figure 2.1).

These mills originally relied on a mix of families living together as well as individuals staying in single-sex dormitory-style housing (Prude 1983). Lowell, in northern Massachusetts at the confluence of the Merrimack and Concord rivers, is a well-studied community that exemplifies the Waltham system. It was one of the first planned industrial cities in America, envisioned as an industrial utopia built on a practical design. As the third incorporated city in Massachusetts, it was strategically placed away from urban areas. Industrialists wanted to ensure that Lowell, and other towns like it, did not develop like European industrial cities, which were overcrowded, unsanitary, and had high unemployment rates (as a result, labor unrest predominated).

Lowell took advantage of the town's surrounding demography to shape and mold an industrial behavior for a new labor force. Unlike middle Atlantic industries, which employed unskilled labor and poor men (Shelton 1986; Wallace 1978), New England industries recruited women and children (Dublin 1977, 1979). Manufacturers' strategy consisted of tapping what they perceived as a new and unexploited labor resource (Marx 1964). Therefore, Lowell's early machine operators consisted primarily of unrelated females from rural communities, often known as mill girls. Their labor was attractive to the corporation since they received much less compensation than their male counterparts (Dublin 1977, 1979; Vogel 1977). Working in these mills appears to be justified, as the corporation implemented a form of corporate paternalism which ensured morality in the factory and in the boardinghouses. Rules and regulations governed the factory system, and industrialist also regulated the worker's leisure time by extending their control to the boardinghouse (Dublin 1977, 1979; Mrozowski, Zeising, and Beaudry 1996; Stansell 1987; Vogel 1977). The mill girls of Lowell published a literary magazine, known as the *Lowell Offering*, which was cited as "an example of the elevated moral attainment of a truly American industrial work force" (Hindle and Lubar 1988:199). The mill girls worked twelve-hour days, six days a week. Bells controlled their daily schedules.

Many industrialists believed that the control of space was as important as the control of time. Manufacturers built uniform housing to reinforce standardized behavior in the domestic setting that could also be implemented in the work force (Faler 1981; Hanlan 1981; Hareven 1978, 1982). In an example from the archaeology at Boott Mills in Lowell, Mrozowski, Zeising, and Beaudry (1996) look at the original eight blocks of the boardinghouses constructed between 1835 and 1839. The company built the factories and boardinghouses with the same design, and each room, usually consisting of two beds, had basically the same type of furnishings. The built environment promoted discipline in the workplace and in the boardinghouse (Beaudry 1989:22; Mrozowski, Zeising, and Beaudry 1996). The houses were arranged at right angles to each other and had facades similar to that of the mill (Beaudry 1987:11; Candee 1992). Industrialists created a similar architectural setting at home as that found in the factory. This similarity helped standardize the built environment and, in return, helped standardize the behavior of the residents in this industrial town. Robinson described the boardinghouses as being extremely attractive; the "best room" had carpet, sometimes

Figure 2.2. Agent's house in Lowell, Massachusetts, 1998. Photograph by Paul A. Shackel.

a piano, and the house manager's "household treasures where callers might be entertained"(Robinson 1976 [1898]: 90–91). Sunday school or church services became mandatory, and prohibitions against the use of alcohol were established. The continued reinforcement of discipline trained people in a new work ethic as standardized behavior created a more efficient work place (Aitken 1985; Hanlan 1981; Hareven 1978, 1982; Zonderman 1992).

In an attempt to display hierarchy, the Kirk Street agents' house, located close to the boardinghouses, was raised above the other structures on an artificial terrace. It had a large back yard separated from the boardinghouses by a wrought-iron fence (Mrozowski, Zeising, and Beaudry 1996:40–42). Agents had large houses with gardens like "paradise," wrote one mill operative (Robinson 1976 [1898]:14). They had flower gardens, with green lawns behind the mills. The mill girls "passed to work through a splendor of dahlias and hollyhocks." Lucy Larcom also mentions the violets, geraniums, green meadows, and so on outside of the mill gates (Larcom 1890:163–164).

The development of the textile industry in the middle Atlantic region differed from that of the large industrial complexes in New England. Cities such as Philadelphia, for example, had many small mills. Until the mid-nineteenth century, the Lowell industries employed unskilled workers and produced standardized coarse cloth, whereas the Philadelphia textile mills relied on skilled handloom weavers, producing specialty items that could not be done by the power loom. The average Philadelphia mill tended to be family-run partnerships with an average of thirty-eight employees, compared to corporations with one thousand employees in Lowell (Hindle and Lubar 1988:202).

It appears that economic considerations may have played a major role in the degree of paternalism found at these places. Eventually, as the cotton market became increasingly competitive and the industry faced several economic downturns, the cost of owning boardinghouses and supporting workers with housing was weighed against profitability and abandoned. By 1850, Lowell was the largest cotton textile center in the nation, but competition with other factories resulted in deteriorating conditions in the factories, as well as at the boardinghouses. The composition of the labor force also changed dramatically. Immigrants left Europe in droves looking for a better life in the United States. Willing to work in the factories for low wages, they replaced the mill girls and became the dominant work force. Capitalists abandoned many of their corporate paternalistic policies, and living and health conditions degenerated.

Lucy Larcom remembered in 1890 her experience as a mill operative earlier in the century and was accepting of the strict paternalism that existed in the mills. "It was a rigid code of morality under which we lived—nobody complained about it, however, and we were doubtless better off for its strictness, in the end," she said (Larcom 1890:181). She supported the idea of corporate paternalism as something necessary. "Even the long hours, early rising, and regularity enforced by the bell were good discipline for one who loved her own personal liberty with a willful rebellion against control" (Larcom 1890:183).

However, other mill operatives, such as Eliza Cate, wrote in 1848 in the *New England Offering*, "Are the factories merely huge piles of neatly arranged bricks, filled with clanking wheels? And are the girls merely automata, moving to and fro as their shuttles move?" (Cate 1848:26–28). A girl leaving the mills and returning home wrote in the *Lowell Offering*, "Where I shall not be obliged to rise so early in the morning, nor be dragged about by the ringing of a bell, nor confined in a close noisy room from morning till night. I will stay here" ("The Spirit of Discontent" 1841:111). These complaints make the workers seem a bit restless and somewhat resistant to the new industrial culture. However, other stories of the exploitation of women in the factories are horrifying. While many of the histories of the Northeast industry glorify the advances of the industrial revolution, managers at Lowell were known

Figure 2.3. Lithograph of Virginius Island with workers' housing (center and V-shape) and Abraham Herr's family's house (below the workers' housing and to the left of the large flour mill, which also was owned by Herr). Courtesy Harpers Ferry National Historical Park.

for sexually abusing the women who worked at the spinning machines in the factories. David Williams (2005:42) describes it as a kind of sex slavery, a practice that was common in the factory system. Women who worked in the factories were tainted for life, as people assumed that managers abused them. Many former factory workers never married and were frequently called "spinsters." It is also curious why some people, like Larcom, felt that they were better off under the control of the corporation while working at Lowell.

Turning to another example, industrialists immediately recognize the value of controlling workers' space and time at work and at home. Another archaeological example can be found at Virginius Island, a small industrial community found adjacent to Harpers Ferry, which is now located in West Virginia. The community began as a small craft community with more than a dozen small, family-owned enterprises. Entrepreneurs placed their small industrial complexes at strategic points on the landscape to access water power rather than follow a development plan. Workers lived nearby and in the adjacent community (Palus and Shackel 2006). However, by the 1850s Abraham Herr owned most of the island, and unlike the previous owners, he subscribed to the model of paternalistic oversight. Controlling workers' living space by standardizing the built environment appears to have been part of Herr's ideal for an industrial community. He constructed a rowhouse for his workers that consisted of a standardized façade, much like the row-houses found in northeastern industrial communities. Archaeology shows that each house had a standardized size and shape on at least the ground floor. Herr built his family's dwelling on the opposite side of the railroad tracks from his mill and the workers' housing, keeping both places within close eyesight of the owner (Palus and Shackel 2006).

The development of the armory at Harpers Ferry is another example of how industrialists changed the built landscape to control and monitor workers. The town developed as a government-operated arms manufac-turing town from the 1790s with civilian workers. Its early built environ-ment demonstrates that the landscapes were transformed according to the needs and expressions of its occupants and the surrounding community. Compared to the Springfield Armory, which was also a government facility, Harpers Ferry lagged in its efficiency and production output. At the same time, it sustained relatively higher production costs (Smith 1977).

In Harpers Ferry, the unstandardized built landscape led to a very dif-ferent type of industrial order when compared to the northern industries. The material and built environment did not reinforce an industrial ethic. Unlike many of the northern industries, the Harpers Ferry Armory had winding roads and individually built factories and domestic housing. This lack of industrial discipline may have been a conscious effort by the indus-trial planners to cater to the craft ideology found in classical republican-ism. Unlike New England industries, which recruited women and children (Dublin 1977, 1979), and middle Atlantic industries, which employed un-skilled labor, immigrants, and poor men (Shelton 1986; Wallace 1978), the Harpers Ferry Armory employed skilled craftsmen. Convincing craftsmen that the new order of industry was justifiable and no threat to their daily routines may have weighed heavily in the decision not to impose rigid fac-tory discipline in the early stages of the armory. By keeping the status quo and by slowly imposing forms of factory discipline, craftsmen were not im-mediately threatened by a modernizing factory system that would alienate their labor and compromise their livelihood. By keeping traditional work ethics and supporting classical republicanism, craftsmen may have been convinced that they could coexist with the new manufacturing system with little or no intrusions made on their everyday lives (Shackel 1996).

In the early nineteenth century, Harpers Ferry armory workers built their own houses, almost anywhere in town, as long as they were outside of the industrial complex. In fact, one worker built his house in the middle of a little-traveled street. Generally, workers and their families could express their own personal identity within the confines of their own homes. Each domestic site excavated shows very different floor plans, and armory workers used a variety of construction materials. The domestic landscape of Harpers Ferry appeared eclectic, unlike the standardized boardinghouses found in the Northeast. Each armory worker family had very different ceramic assemblages, which is an expression of each household's individuality, a phenomenon that disappeared in Harpers Ferry by the late nineteenth century (Lucas 1994; Lucas and Shackel 1994; Palus and Shackel 2006; Shackel 2000a).

The armory workers defied any attempt to unify them as a work force and resisted the industrial process much longer than their counterparts in Springfield, Massachusetts. Supervisors made it difficult for northerners who tried to introduce new mechanized processes, and the armory superintendent gave very little support to John Hall, a gun maker from Maine working in Harpers Ferry as he perfected the process of interchangeable parts. New time-saving machinery was slowly introduced to the armory worker in the 1830s and 1840s, and by the 1840s the armorers had lost their power and were forced to become wage laborers if they wanted to be employed. The federal government imposed a factory system and redesigned the town to include standardized architecture between the domestic dwellings and factories. In addition, a grid town plan was imposed over the town and a military superintendent replaced a civilian one. The workers protested, but without success (Shackel 1996:106–109). The archaeological record shows that at least in one case, armorers practiced their craft in a piecework system at home until about 1841, when the military took over control of the facility and made all workers abide by a standard work discipline found in industries throughout the country. After 1841, armory work was no longer performed in a domestic context (Shackel 1996, 1999a, 1999b).

Armory craftsmen protested these conditions as they became what they had always feared—tenders of machinery. On the household level, where women took charge of consumerism, an interesting pattern develops in the archaeological record. Those with a head of household in charge of the wage-labor operations, such as the master armorer, were eager to purchase the newest and most fashionable commodities transported into town by rail and canal, both established at Harpers Ferry in the mid-1830s. In contrast, an armory worker's household was reluctant to acquire new consumer goods. They acquired and used consumer goods that had been fashionable several generations earlier (Lucas and Shackel 1994). Much in the same way that residents longed for their craft occupation, the archaeological findings from a worker's family shows a material culture expression that was commonly found in the town's preindustrial order—an era when families had more control over their daily and work lives (Shackel 1996).

The archaeobotanical analysis of pollen and phytoliths remains at Harpers Ferry shows the deterioration of the town's industrial landscape from the 1840s, when there was increased governmental paternalism. Analysis indicates that the pre-1830s landscape shows the presence of grasses throughout the town. Apparently, during an era characterized by task-oriented labor and an unplanned town and factory system, the government paid particular attention to landscaping and created a pastoral-like setting next to a major industrial complex. Once the military took control of the working operations, created a factory discipline, and tried to control the domestic lives of workers and their families, the grasses disappeared and were replaced by weeds (Cummings 1994:94–105; Rovner 1994:37–48). Industry and work discipline took precedence over maintaining the landscape and industrialists no longer needed to justify the coexistence of the machine within the garden.

In another example, the company coal-mining town of Berwind, Colorado, owned and controlled by Colorado Fuel and Iron Company (CF&I), developed a sociology department, which established material strategies to standardize and Americanize their work force. Until 1901 workers could build their own housing, and homes usually consisted of low-cost materials or items that could be scavenged: wood, stone, corrugated metal sheeting, flattened tin cans, mud, and so on. In many cases, workers could build their homes or take up residence where they liked in the community, and they often settled adjacent to others of similar ethnic background. But in 1902 the corporation's weekly publication started to criticize the community's vernacular housing as unsafe and unsanitary. The company began to standardize its workers' housing with common architectural features. Small, concrete-block cottages sprang up in neat rows. The corporation also placed families close to unfamiliar ethnic groups, a strategy meant to curb communication and impede collaborative action. In 1901, only 12 percent of the families had no ethnic affiliation with their neighbors, but by 1910 this had increased to 41 percent. The company would also purposefully mix nationalities in the mines so that they could not communicate and organize (Saitta 2007:51–53; Wood 2002). The superintendent's house, along with the school, was strategically placed on a hill at the north end of the camp. The Catholic and Protestant churches sat next to the mining administration building in the center of the camp, making a connection between the corporation and religious authority (Saitta 2007:52).

The iron plantation at Hopewell, established in 1771, is on the upper reaches of French Creek, north of Philadelphia. Now a national historic park, the archaeology and reconstructions show the industrial works and community that comprised this iron plantation. Boardinghouses and tenant houses harbored the workers and their families. The village lacks any formal street design, and it may seem like an unplanned community. On the contrary, the ironmaster's house was strategically placed. It was close to the industrial complex, where he could observe the work process, and he had a view of the workers' houses and could observe their daily activities (Kemper n.d.; NPS 1983; Sharp and Thomas 1966).

Other archaeologists have also explored the relationship between the corporate town and paternalistic oversight. In the American Southwest, many of the company mining towns and large labor encampments from the late nineteenth century followed a grid pattern that reflected order and rationality, while the smaller towns formed in linear strips along roadways. Such strategies allowed owners to easily account for their work force. Hardesty's (1988:13–14, 88; 1998) work in the American West provides considerable attention to the composition of settlements and households, and he shows that hierarchy and power are explicit in town layouts, general settlement patterns, and the mining complexes of the West. In his study of the town of McGill in eastern Nevada, Hardesty shows how hierarchy played out on the landscape: high-ranking officials occupied the "Circle," middle managers the "middle town," and workers the "lower town."

Work camps are some of the most common archaeological signatures found around industrial sites. While kinship and tribute played a role in the development of the earliest work camps, by the nineteenth century wage labor and industrial capitalism was influencing how these communities developed. Also, class, gender, and ethnicity shaped hierarchy and class relations at these places (Hardesty 2002:94). Beginning in the 1880s and continuing until World War II, for instance, copper dominated the mining in Arizona. Anglo-Irish miners and labor unions worked hard to marginalize Mexican and southern European workers. Mining communities were often separated into "white" and "Mexican" camps (Sheridan 1998:174). Baxter (2002:22) also shows how industrial and domestic landscapes were developed and separated into professional and domestic, public and private spaces with the development of Squaw Flat oil field in the early twentieth century.

Pappas (2004:159–176) describes a work camp site established in the Sierra Nevada Mountains of California in 1955 called Soap Creek Pass. Corporate paternalism helped to create a network of fictitious kin relationships that could be defined through residence patterns, social status, and corporate morality. Paternalism also was accompanied by a form of surveillance whereby managers resided on a hill above the workers. However, unlike many other company towns, the residents of Soap Creek Pass were allowed to personalize their residence as long as they did not change the basic structure.

Randall McGuire (1988, 1991) shows the changing strategies used by capitalists in late-nineteenth- and early-twentieth-century Binghamton, New York. For instance, in the 1880s Jonas Kilmer constructed his industrial empire by creating a landscape that reinforced his power. He built a new swamp-root cure factory that dominated the view of the railroad passengers' depot in Binghamton. It was the first building visitors saw when they entered town. He also placed his dwelling at the end of mansion row. Built with two massive towers, it presented the image of a fortification. The Kilmer mausoleum is also on the highest point in the cemetery and is larger than many of the apartments that Kilmer's workers inhabited (McGuire 1988; 1991:108–113). A crisis in capitalism throughout the country at the turn of the century made it necessary for George F. Johnson, another local entrepreneur, to create a very different landscape in the early twentieth century. He downplayed inequalities by creating an industrial welfare system. Company profits were used in the community to build hospitals, parks, and public monuments. Johnson's house escapes the ostentation that was prevalent decades earlier and his gravesite is far less elaborate than Kilmer's. The landscape masked class inequities and created an illusion of equality between labor and capital (McGuire 1991:114–123).

Some Thoughts

With the development of the industrial revolution, industrialists created new surveillance technologies to monitor and control a work force that was increasingly being paid a wage rather than for work by the piece. One strategy was to place workers under one roof so that the capitalists could control the space and monitor their workers. Carefully planned landscapes helped control a growing and impoverished work force in both the factory and the town. A large, landless working class became the industrial work force that led to urbanized centers, which became known as the workshops of the world. Those areas that could make the transition became industrial centers, while those that did not change their mode of production were outcompeted by their more efficient and lower-priced rivals (Wolf 1982:267). Capitalists also developed a variety of techniques to control the daily lives of workers at home and create a docile work force, the major topic of the next chapter. While industrialists abandoned some of these strategies, some form of surveillance was important for the continued success of controlling workers. This is visible in the remaining industrial landscapes and is clear from the evidence in many of the archeological excavations.

3

Workers' Housing in
the Late Nineteenth Century

Late-Nineteenth-Century Boarding

Boardinghouses became popular in urban areas where companies or keepers supplied both room and board to occupants. Archaeology at Lowell, Massachusetts, shows that by the end of the nineteenth century, the paternal philosophy for operating the boardinghouses, whereby owners influenced and to some extent controlled the domestic lives of the mill girls, had disappeared. Susan Strasser (1982:148), known for her work *Never Done: A History of American Housework*, remarks that the growth of boardinghouses in urban areas was a direct outgrowth of the development of a wage-labor system. By 1860 boarding was so common in the United States that one historian noted that "nearly all Americans lived in hotels or boarding-houses" during this era (Strasser 1982:148; Martin 1942:148–149). Americans who chose not to stay at boardinghouses could stay at hotels, where they could also receive meals. These hotel accommodations with room and board were called the American plan (Strasser 1982:148). But for the most part, industrial workers and their families found refuge in low-cost boardinghouse arrangements.

By the third quarter of the nineteenth century, boardinghouse architecture had changed significantly in urban areas such as New York. The earlier structures were usually wooden subdivided houses, which by the mid-nineteenth century were dilapidated and in generally poor condition. During the 1850s, 1860s, and 1870s, middle-class boardinghouses were generally converted rowhouses with brownstone fronts. An 1869 *New York Times* article noted the deceptive character of these new boardinghouses. Reinforcing xenophobic fears, the article claimed that while they looked like private dwellings from the street, within them was a mixture of strangers and the seeds of destruction of family life (Cromley 1989:25).

Charles Henderson (1897:46) wrote, "The boarding-house of a city is not seldom a dreary place, furnishing room and meals as a mere business transaction without any of those elements of companionship, which make up our idea of home." In 1871, another *New York Times* (August 6, 1871:5) article commented on dining in public places and noted that "if private family dinners should give way to eating in public, family values might be diminished, if not lost" (quoted in Cromley 1989:24). With the loss of domestic input and the public conditions of the boardinghouse, women in these situations neglected the domestic duties that nineteenth-century society expected of them.

A contemporary New Yorker found living in a "boarding house, at its best, is but a miserable mockery of a home." Another citizen commented that a boardinghouse had "nothing like comfort or content anywhere, but the opposite of what you mean when you talk of home" (Cromley 1989:21). T. Butler Gunn described for *Harpers Weekly* (October 10, 1857:652) the conditions of a lower-class boardinghouse in New York City, the same conditions found in other urban areas:

> His bed lacks blankets; the sheets pieced and torn; one of the chairs is unsound. Meals in such a house are funereal ceremonies. The staple of food is tough steak sawed into fragments by the landlady; this is eaten in solemn silence, in mourning for the meal. Breakfast is composed of steak, warm water with a flavor of bad coffee hovering over it, chunks of unleavened bread, and butter which is half-way cheese. Dinner is steak, as before, veal or roast beef, the latter in such extraordinary cuts that one is forced to the conclusion that a deformed ox has been sacrificed for the repast, pie—eaten with a knife and cheese but no fork—and perhaps a cup of tepid water discolored with tea-leaves and chalk. (Gunn 1857:652)

R. Vashon Rogers, an etiquette book author and visitor to one of these establishments, described the meal of poultry served there, painting an unappetizing picture:

> Every kind of finer tendon and ligament that is in the nature of poultry to possess was developed in these specimens in the singular form of guitar strings. Their limbs appear to have struck roots into their breasts and bodies, as aged trees strike roots into the earth. Their legs were so hard as to encourage the idea that they must have devoted the greater part of their long and arduous lives to pedestrian exercises and

the walking of matches. No one could have cleaned the drum stick
without being of ostrich descent. (Rogers 1884:152–153)

Describing the tea served at the boardinghouse, Rogers (1884:166) sarcasti-
cally noted, "The tea was none of that good stuff that once brought $50 a
pound, but some of the adulterated mixture, thirty million pounds of which
Uncle Sam, Aunt Columbia and their little ones, pour annually into their
saucers and empty into their mouths."

In the *Harper's New Monthly Magazine* (1882:112–113), an article titled
"Money-Making for Ladies," described the work of a boardinghouse keeper
as one of the most difficult jobs for a woman to undertake in order to make
extra money. Operations required "the gift of economy." The author provides
tips on the how to accommodate guests with good meals without skimping.
The article also commented on the lodging: "How often, for instance, does
any one looking for board chance to find a room that has a home look about
it? Do not the apartments generally shown look as if some one had just
died there, and everything has been dismantled in consequence" ("Money-
Making for Ladies" 1882:113).

In 1899, S. T. Rorer (1899:29) acknowledged in the *Ladies' Home Journal*
that the conditions of the boardinghouse were not necessarily the fault of
the boardinghouse mistress, who in most cases was trying to eke out a living. Tenants expected too much for their money, he noted, and thought
they should feast every night: "People complain, not because the food is
bad, but because it seems to be natural to complain about and criticize the
boarding-house table" (Rorer 1899:29). While most families ate meat once
a day, boardinghouse residents expected it three times a day. Because of
newly developed transportation systems, most people in large cities were
accustomed to having the freshest vegetables and meats. But when they left
the city for the summer and stayed at a boardinghouse, Rorer noted, they
encountered their "first surprise—inferior meats badly cooked, vegetables
that have been kept all winter long; a perfectly natural thing under the existing conditions" (Rorer 1899:29).

The article stated that generally, the boardinghouse keeper was an un-
trained housewife in need of earning a living, even though she was not "especially adapted to it" (Rorer 1899:26). Servants in the boardinghouse were
also not very well trained and tended to be wasteful, Rorer noted. Lodgers
always tried to get their money's worth at boardinghouses, but they often
forgot the expenses of servants, fuel, rent, and wear and tear on the furni-

ture. On the whole, boardinghouse keepers did not make much of a living; rather, they survived a "miserable existence" (Rorer 1899:26).

The archaeological research at Lowell reveals other conditions associated with boardinghouse life. For instance, while public water and sanitation was available in the 1870s to the agents' homes, many of the boardinghouses still used well water and privies through the 1890s (Mrozowski 2006:142–143). The unequal access to health and sanitation in the communities reinforced class differences in the degrading neighborhoods. The identified faunal bones found in this back yard show that the occupants' diet consisted of a staple of cow, pig, sheep, goat, and chicken. Rodents gnawed on these bones, which is one piece of evidence that shows the deteriorating conditions of the back yards as trash was scattered throughout the area. The evidence provides an image of rodents roaming freely through boardinghouse back yards feeding on trash. Parasites in the fecal material found in privies and the presence of lice combs are also telling of the poor sanitary conditions. The pollen record show that grassy and well-manicured back yards of the early boardinghouse era was replaced by a weedy and unkempt landscape by the late nineteenth century (Mrozowski, Zeising, and Beaudry 1996).

Liquor bottles were also found in the boardinghouse back yard. These items tend to be small objects from local manufacturers. The smaller liquor bottles were cheaper than larger ones, they were easy to conceal, and their presence implies immediacy of use. The presence of these items in the back yard, next to the privy, also shows that the users tried to conceal their practice from household members, boardinghouse keepers, or the agent (Mrozowski, Zeising, and Beaudry 1996).

Little and Kassner (2001:62) discuss another way to look at these urban assemblages with large amounts of bottle glass, bones, and button. They show (citing Praetzellis and Praetzellis 1990:396) that junking was a major part of the nineteenth-century economy, especially among the poor. Clothes were collected for resale or for rags and they were sold to brokers who sold them to paper or cloth mill, where the rags were shredded, spun, and rewoven into "shoddy cloth." Little and Kassner conclude, therefore, that the high number of buttons found near alley dwellings in Washington, D.C., may be a byproduct of the collection of rags and served as an economic sideline for the household. The high quantity of bottle glass found in back yards is not necessarily a sign of an unkempt landscape or a reflection of excessive drinking; rather, the materials may have served as a family's bank account. The bottles were collected in order to be resold and recycled. Bones could also be saved in order to be later recycled to produce meal for fertilizer or to serve as blanks for the manufacture of buttons (Little and Kassner 2001:62).

Tenement Living and Working-Class People

Many of the archaeological studies related to domestic life in industrial settings are often centered on boardinghouse life. There are a few published archeological examples of tenement housing and the conditions of daily life as a result of capitalism and the impact of industrialization. The exhaustive work at Five Points in New York City helps to fill this gap (Yamin 1998, 2001, 2002). Also, *The Archaeology of Urban Landscapes: Explorations in Slumland* (Mayne and Murry, eds. 2001) focuses on this deficiency. These works explore the diversity of cultures and variety of households that once lived in urban industrialized areas.

In Alan Mayne and Tim Murry's (2001:1) introduction, they infer that the term "slum" originated in the nineteenth century. They believe that archaeology can provide a more varied view of working-class urban living by providing agency to the individuals living in these areas, and thus the label "slum" is an outsider's term and not justifiable. In this case, I believe the search for agency follows a slippery slope. Relativizing poverty is a weapon of the modern capitalist system and understates the living and working conditions that the new immigrant and the working class faced. While studies of agency have given working-class people a presence in the archaeological and historical record, in this case the claim for agency understates some of the serious issues of the past and the present, such as poverty, poor nutrition, lack of education, and various forms of slavery, such as industrial, domestic, and sex. The urban poor have limited choices and have a difficult time gaining the simple advantages in life, such as education, health care, and living wages.

While it is difficult to associate the general topic of tenement life with a particular industry, the residents were working-class people and often associated with some form of labor. They were usually employed in sweatshops or cottage industries. They also worked as laborers or domestic help. The rise of tenement living is associated with the need of groups of people in urban areas who worked for substandard wages to find affordable living places (Figure 3.1). The tenement allowed for industrialists and business owners to maintain low wages and seek greater profits. Looking at the development

Figure 3.1. Tenement house in New York City. *Harper's Weekly*, September 13, 1873, 796.

of tenement living allows for this history of domestic life for working-class people.

Tenements are often considered the apartment house of the poor. They have been traditionally defined as a place of residence with three or more families living separately and doing their cooking on the premise (DeForest and Veiller 1970:37). Tenements in large cities had few conveniences. A social reformer called the people living in these crowded conditions "cliff-dwellers," those "who must sleep, cook, eat wash, iron in one to three rooms" (Henderson 1897:84). Generally, reformers believed that these tenements were a growing source of immorality and disease (Yamin 2000:338–370). Robert DeForest and Lawrence Veiller (1970:80) depict of the worst tenements in New York as "squalid wretchedness, intemperance, and filth."

Health reformers of the late nineteenth and early twentieth centuries believed that society should be able to supply housing to the poor, even with some "objectionable . . . features," rather than not supply any housing at all (van der Bent 1917:299). Two of the strongest proponents of the family, Catherine Beecher and Harriet Beecher Stowe (1994 [1869]), proposed building affordable, healthy, and safe housing for the poor. Their 1869 publication and their position in healthy and affordable housing is best reviewed in the context of New York's Tenement House Act of 1867. Room ventilation concerned the authors of the act, since tenement residents had a high disease rate. Many tenement apartments contained bedrooms without exterior or interior windows. The act required every habitable room to have a window, and landlords responded by cutting windows in interior rooms for ventilation. One contemporary physician remarked in 1870, "If we could see the air breathed by these poor creatures in their tenements it would show itself to be fowler [sic] than the mud of the gutters" (Riis 1970:14). The amount of space in the rear yard was regulated by the act, and cesspools were banned from areas adjacent to the building.

Beecher and Stowe (1994 [1869]) proposed that living in tenements was an acceptable form of a living arrangement as long as the apartments had a proper warming and ventilation system, a standard deficiency in contemporary tenements. In most tenement situations the family could be self-contained and family morals could be more easily taught than in a boardinghouse situation. Since the tenements were built up against each other, side by side, they lacked windows in the core of the buildings. Therefore, Beecher and Stowe (1994 [1869]) proposed four symmetrical apartments with a central hall corridor dividing the apartments, two on each side. Each would have a parlor, twenty foot square, with a bedroom and a kitchen toward the interior, and each would be equipped with trash flues and a dumb waiter. The parlor would be the only room in each apartment with windows facing the exterior. Toward the interior of the apartment, and adjacent to the central hall corridor, there would be a ventilating recess from the basement to the roof and widows from the bedroom opening into the shaft in order to secure light and air. A sliding door would separate the kitchen and bedroom from the parlor. They suggested that the parlor sliding doors be glazed from top to bottom in order to give light to the other two rooms (Beecher and Stowe 1994 [1869]:441–446). Such an apartment, the authors said, could easily house a family of four. The adjacent apartment could be appended, with a sliding glass door into that apartment, converting the kitchen into a bedroom and thus housing a family of ten (446).

In the winter of 1878–79, *The Plumber and Sanitary Engineer* ran a contest in search for the best tenement design. The publication required that the building conform to a standard lot twenty-five by one hundred feet in size, be safe, and allow for maximum profit for the landlord. The winning design, published in the March 1879 issue of the journal, became known as the "dumbbell" because of its designed shape. It had an indenture in the middle and at both sides of the building. These indentures allowed each room to have a window, a practice not adhered to by earlier tenement landlords. This feature quickly became a necessity because the 1879 New York City housing law required windows in every room (Jackson 1984:325). The indenture also allowed landlords to build the tenements up against each other with minimum loss of space. The average dumbbell was divided into four apartments per floor and stood six stories high. It also contained two water closets per floor. Contemporaries hailed it a success because it allowed light and air to each apartment through the shaft on the central exterior wall.

By the turn of the century, two-thirds of New York City's 3.5 million people lived in dumbbell tenements, aggravating the city's overpopulation problem. In 1910, New York passed the Tenement House Law, which outlawed the dumbbell and set the standard for housing legislation in the United States. Besides health and safety codes, it also required that new tenements be placed on larger lots with a fifty-foot minimum width and that building land coverage be limited to 70 percent. This allowed for increased ventilation and light for each apartment. It remains the basic code for low-rise housing in much of the country today (Jackson 1984:326; Tunick 1986:4).

While reform was underway in housing, not everyone hailed these new advancements in health and safety for the poor. Teunis J. van der Bent wrote in 1917 in an architectural guide for planning apartment houses that although health and safety issues should not be ignored, "if in detail and finish various demands may be made in order to obtain sanitary or hygienic construction, there should be a limit to same in order to avoid even the appearance of extravagance or waste" (van der Bent 1917:299). Van der Bent claimed that New York's Tenement House Law made it too costly to find landlords willing to abide by all of the regulations. He noted that "the New

York Tenement House Law, carried a little further, will some day prescribe for the tenants the use of three pronged forks in the place of four pronged forks, or ordinances of a similar nature" (van der Bent 1917:300).

Social reformers also wrote housekeeping books for families living in tenements (Kittredge 1911). Housekeeping advisors believed that flats and tenements were an economical form of living. Living in such an arrangement, the housewife could perform all of her duties much quicker than if she had to care for two or more floors. They believed that the smaller domicile was especially advantageous for a working woman (Parloa 1893:18).

Since tenements tended to be dark, guide books prescribed that all the rooms be painted yellow. The floors should be stained and cleaned with "soapy water, to which add a little kerosene as a disinfectant" (Kittredge 1911:10). As a way to "Americanize" the poor and the new immigrant, the guide books also explained that each bedroom should have shelves enclosed with curtains if no closet was furnished. Housekeeping classes were developed for tenement dwellers and included such topics as the care of stoves, making morning fires in the range, dishwashing, cooking, setting the table, and various other housework tasks (Kittredge 1911:14).

While these guidelines were prescribed ideals, they were usually unobtainable for working-class families living in tenements. And although the lack of privacy was seen in an unfavorable light by Victorian reformers, Christine Stansell (1987:46–52) claims that a somewhat communal life-style created closer bonds among women, thus aiding their family's survival.

Generally, children were sent to work or to scavenge and salvage for their families. This type of work may have created the "bank accounts" of recyclable clothing, buttons, bottle glass, and bones often found around tenements (Little and Kassner 2001). Boydston (1990:92) notes that given the circumstances that working-class families faced, "what is striking about antebellum working-class mothers is not their failure, but their remarkable success in finding ways to care for their children."

While middle-class reformers tried to set guidelines for tenement dwellers, these areas should also be seen as places of working-class radicalism and places that resisted the dominant culture. The stories of Five Points (Yamin 1998:74–85) provide many vignettes of life in mid-nineteenth-century New York tenement living. Rebecca Yamin (1998:83) describes the shanties and tenements that lined the streets, packed by families trying to eke out a living: "Death and despair did their work without fanfare . . . and they did a lot of it; just walking down those lonely, decrepit streets was enough to make the sunniest of souls wonder about the ultimate value of human life" (Yamin

1998:83). About one hundred people crammed into 472 Pearl Street, a five-story building and a smaller four-story brick tenement in the backlot. More than half of the Irish immigrants living in the area worked as unskilled laborers, while the remainder had trades or semiskilled occupations (Fitts 2000:69–71).

The archaeology at one Five Points tenement filled with Irish immigrants shows that the residents maintained tea drinking as part of their daily routines. The Irish laborers tended to favor eating pork rather than less expensive fish dishes. Hams, steaks, hocks, and pigs feet were stewed for hours in wines and spices. While archaeologists found evidence of alcohol consumption, the residents used a significantly greater amount of medicines. The presence of glass syringes indicates the use of the addictive pain-killing drug morphine (Yamin 1998:78–80). Lice combs indicate that the residents had a need and probably a desire to maintain good hygiene (Fitts 2000:102).

While some industrialists exercised their powers to make a difference in creating social capital in workers' communities, others ignored the benefits of providing for workers. However, towns such as Pullman, Illinois, Goodyear Heights, Ohio, and Tyrone, New Mexico, are important examples of the new welfare capitalism that developed during the Progressive era (Metheny 2007:4–5).

George Pullman established a railroad-car manufacturing facility and a town named after him in what is now Chicago's Far South Side during the early 1880s. As an answer to the urban blight that was affecting major industrial centers, the town of Pullman had shared community spaces, well-manicured, pastoral-like landscapes, and community buildings, such as shops, libraries, theaters, and police and fire departments. Workers lived in rowhouses, the higher status workers having larger accommodations (Figure 3.2). Pullman believed that decent pay and descent living conditions could solve labor unrest. Many saw the town of more than eight thousand residents as an industrial utopia that could improve the plight of the working class. People came to visit this social experiment and the workers and their families were on continuous display. Outsiders pondered whether these amenities could improve the morality of the laboring class (Baxter 2007).

Excavations by Jane Baxter (2007) found two discrete deposits that reveal an interesting story of class and social separations in Pullman. In the factory yards, near one of the transfer pits, she identified discrete deposits where eating and drinking occurred. Inexpensive whiteware ceramics, cheap soda water bottles, and low-cost meat cuts from chicken and pork were the most

Figure 3.2. Rowhouses in the Pullman district, originally constructed by George Pullman for workers and their families. Photograph by Paul A. Shackel, 2007.

common artifacts in this assemblage. The assemblage is evidence that workers were taking breaks or eating their lunch in a workspace behind the factory. In contrast, the archaeological assemblage near the former location of the Corliss steam engine provides a different story.

On display at the 1876 Centenary Exhibition in Philadelphia, the engine was an example of "modern" technology. Pullman purchased the engine and moved it to a location behind the factory. It powered all the industry of his car works and heated all the homes and structures in the community. Excavations around the location of the Corliss steam engine suggest that the engine continued to be a curiosity. Baxter (2007) found a brick walkway around the engine, along with fragments of a gold, gilded porcelain teacup. These fragments are from the most expensive teawares found in Pullman, including the domestic sites in town. This archaeological signature suggests that visitors came to see the Corliss steam engine and were treated to tea in fine porcelain cups as they viewed the technological marvel. Additionally, while the workers in the factory labored and followed a time discipline, visitors were observing their neighborhoods.

Pullman's dream for a utopian community fell apart in 1894. The Panic of 1893 led to decreased demand for the train cars, and Pullman's company cut wages by 28 percent. Workers complained that rents did not decrease, but their complaints fell on deaf ears. The workers went on strike and were supported by the American Railroad Union. They refused to handle any trains with Pullman cars. When the strike was over, Pullman was villainized and remained unpopular with labor until his death in 1897. The following year the Illinois Supreme Court ordered that the company divest ownership of the town (Zinn 2003:279–281). Today, Pullman is a quiet residential area of Far South Chicago with about 95 percent of the town still standing. Part of the factory complex is also still standing, but it is not open to public.

One industrialist, George McMurtry (1838–1915), a steel master from Pittsburgh, created the model town of Vandergrift, about forty miles northeast of the city, which eventually became nationally visible as an experiment in industrial reform. He used Fredrick Law Olmsted's firm to design the town, which included private home ownership. For each model town constructed in the United States in the late nineteenth century, there were scores of other communities that developed in a haphazard way. In 1896, McMurtry sold the first lots, and Vandergrift, Pennsylvania, stood out as one of only a few model communities in the industrial Northeast (Mosher 1995:84). Having spent about two decades dealing with labor issues and occasional striking workers, and following some of the most violent strikes in America, including the Great Railroad Strike of 1877, Haymarket Riot of 1886, Homestead Strike of 1892, and Pullman Strike of 1894, McMurtry visited model industrial towns in Europe. These town plans had comprehensively planned infrastructures and adequate light and ventilation in houses, and factories successfully used landscapes and the built environment to maintain control over labor. He used these ideals in his town planning, which helped him subvert unionization in the steel industry at large (Mosher 1995:84–89).

Some industrialists such as McMurtry believed that well-planned living environments would make better citizens and better workers because the laborers would feel gratitude for the industrialist who created these better conditions (Mosher 1995:91). McMurtry's workers were so loyal to him, in fact, that he successfully used them to break one of the first strikes waged against the entire system of mills owned by the Unites States Steel Corporation. When a call for a unionized strike arose in 1901, the workers in Vandergrift refused to join. Those from Vandergrift testified that they received good wages, steady employment, and lived in a "moral and modern town" (Mosher 1995:101). David Harvey (1978, quoted in Mosher 1995:104) explains that "by encouraging workers to become petty proprietors through home ownership, McMurtry succeeded in aligning the goals of labor with those of capital and simultaneously inserted capital's power into the landscape via the inertial properties of home ownership. Homeowners expressed little interest in striking or organizing so long as they held property or a mortgage on it."

Some Thoughts

There are a significant number of studies that include a description of working-class life at boardinghouses and tenements. In most cases the living conditions were horrendous at best. Working-class people lived in overcrowded buildings, they often suffered with poor diets and health conditions, and there was little time for their children to acquire an education. While this chapter focuses on the urban East Coast, the daily living conditions of working-class households in other areas of the country were poor as capitalists underpaid and undervalued their workers and a new immigrant workforce was willing to work and live in substandard conditions and compete for low-paying jobs.

By the end of the nineteenth century, Americans were taking notice of the declining urban conditions in the industrial Northeast. Populist politicians blamed the conditions on the urban-based oligarchy of capitalist financiers who profited from industry and the expense of workers. Others blamed politicians for regulating industries, since only capital could achieve long-term progress. Nativists accused the new immigrants, including Roman Catholics, socialists, and anarchists, for disrupting the Protestant ethic. Middle-class reformers viewed the chaotic, unnatural, and unsanitary living conditions that severely impacted the urban industrial worker as the cause of the problem (Mosher 1995:90). Solutions ranged from radical socialist revolutions to more conservative approaches that slightly modified capitalism. These reforms, which became widely adopted, included providing more affordable services to workers, including the municipalization of electricity, sewage, and water systems (Mosher 1995:90–91).

However, many of these concessions were not easily acquired. Many workers resisted the new industrial work culture, individually or collectively, through sabotage, work slow-downs, and strikes. The following chapter provides an overview of some of these resistance movements, and I show how archeologists are helping to make these events and issues part of the national public memory.

4

Power, Resistance, and Alternatives

The use of power—who uses it and how it is used—is an important concept for understanding social relations in an industrial setting. Power is not simply repressive or the domination of one group over another. It can be positive and a productive form of knowledge. There are multiple centers of power, and power can be found at many levels—in the institution, within the community, or within the family. It is seen in all social relations and permeates every aspect of social interaction (Foucault 1977). Daniel Miller and Christopher Tilley (1984) describe power in two forms—*power to* and *power over*. *Power to* is part of all social action and can take the form of authority. All people have access to practical power. It is a coercive power that people or groups follow because they believe it is for the good of the social order. For instance, people who believe the authority figure (either business owner or clergy) who tells them that they are lucky to have a wage, that if they work hard enough they will overcome poverty and oppression, and that if they do not strike they will be entitled to a better afterlife will not strike. *Power over* is about social control and domination. It is a repressive power that is used by institutions to ensure subservience to the social order. This type of power comes with the control of strategic resources, which forms the basis for social control (Shanks and Tilley 1992:129; Saitta 2007:23). A form of industrial slavery in which workers have no choice but to labor in factories or iron furnaces may be an example of such power. The workers do not control their freedom, nor do they have the ability to easily change their status. Therefore, power can produce or repress social action. It is not a centralized, repressing resistance in discrete locations; rather, power can dilute resistance along power networks embedded in the social order (Foucault 1980:119).

The ideals of capitalism found in liberal republicanism did not necessarily spread evenly from one community to another. While power is present with the development of industrial society and the creation of workers, people either resisted or accepted these changes. Reactions varied, sometimes according to community, class, and gender (Gilje 1996:170; Little 1997). What follows are a few examples of how archaeologists have identified resistance in the new industrial order.

Resistance in the Workplace

In the early nineteenth century, ideologies related to modernizing industrial conditions and the formation of a working-class society developed. Industrialists and workers often had different views about labor, and factory owners often characterized unproductive workers as unreliable, careless, or lazy. Many scholars interpret this lackadaisical behavior as a deliberate attempt to resist the dominance of a machine-based system of production that left operatives with little room for personal autonomy or craft pride (Prude 1983; Scott 1990). While craftsmen often owned their own means of production and were likely to treat them with care, factory workers had little loyalty to the machines someone else owned. "Some workers," notes Zonderman (1992:48), "abused their machinery to show that they had little traditional pride in or attachment to their machines or to the products they made." Workers broke machinery through various acts of sabotage in an effort to reassert the primacy of human beings over machines (Juravich 1985; Paynter 1989:386; Paynter and McGuire 1991; Scott 1985; Shackel 1996:59–61).

Goods were sometimes stolen from the mills and factories, even though operatives knew that they could be fired if caught. Yet pilfering was seen as a way to "even the score" and compensate for low wages: "If they were denied what they saw as the full value of their labor, they would find a way to get what they thought was due them" (Zonderman 1992:196). Operatives were also rumored to have taken revenge by setting fires to factories. While they might have lost their jobs in such cases, they easily could have found another one at a factory in a neighboring town. In one instance, suspicious fires occurred at the Springfield Armory in 1842 when the armory management was shifted from civilian to military control. Neither the armorers nor the surrounding community helped to extinguish the fires (Zonderman 1992:196).

Factory workers' search for freedom and their expression of grievances against entrepreneurs were expressed from the outset of the industrial era by quitting and moving to other jobs rather than staying and fighting for change to alleviate the boredom, tedium, and low wages of factory labor. In some ways the workers' transient state undermined their stability and strength, as they lacked the cohesiveness for social and labor change. This does not mean that protests were nonexistent. They occurred, but often they were less collective and less overt than strikes. The earliest organized strike at a large manufacturing company in the United States occurred at Waltham, Massachusetts, in 1821, catalyzed by a reduction in wages. One mechanic wrote, "The girls as one revolted, and the work stopped for two days in consequence" (Hindle and Lubar 1988:201). In 1824, female weavers in Pawtucket, Rhode Island, led a strike against lower wages and increased hours. In this case the owners closed the factory for two weeks and a portion of one of the mills was set on fire. In December 1829, mill operatives in Dover, New Hampshire, walked off their jobs on a Friday because of "obnoxious regulations." They fired guns in the street and were released from their jobs by the mill owners, but they were back on the jobs the following Monday without any concessions made by the owners. Other known strikes occurred throughout the decade, and in many cases workers returned to their jobs without any substantial gains (Zonderman 1992:197ff).

By the 1830s and 1840s, regional labor organizations became more powerful in the Northeast. New strategies were used to gain the sympathy of workers, community, and mill owners for concessions. In Lowell, for instance, operatives in an 1834 strike rooted their actions in the tradition of the American Revolution. They called themselves the "daughters of freemen" and invoked the traditional ideals of respect, justice, and equity. At the same time they called their employers "purse-proud aristocrats." By calling themselves the "daughters of freemen," they drew attention to the dangers of factory bondage. They no longer wanted the role of dutiful daughter to their paternalistic managers in the mill structure. It was imperative that workers unite in order to gain more labor freedoms (Dublin 1977, 1979; Foner 1977; Prude 1983; Hindle and Lubar 1988:163; Stansell 1987; Vogel 1977; Zonderman 1992:197–203). However, not all of the mill girls were united about striking. One operative noted that she believed participating in strikes against mill tyrants made the workers tyrants too (Larcom 1970 [1875]:118).

The leader of the Workingman's Party in Massachusetts exclaimed in his *Address to the Workingmen of New England*, "Let us be determined no longer to be deceived by the cry of those who produce nothing and enjoy all, and who insultingly term us—the farmers, the mechanics, and laborers—the LOWER ORDER—while the DECLARATION OF INDEPENDENCE asserts that 'ALL MEN ARE CREATED EQUAL'" (Hindle and Lubar 1988:163–164). The parallel between America's fight for liberty and workers' struggle to control their labor dominated the outcries in the first several decades of the American industrial revolution. One versifier wrote,

For liberty our fathers fought
Which with their blood they dearly bought,
The Fact'ry system sets at nought. . . .
Great Britain curse is now our own,
Enough to damn a King and Throne. (Prude 1983:120)

The shift and struggle from craft to industry continued into the early twentieth century (Fonse-Wolf 1996:28–49). And when workers were not powerful enough to organize a strike, they protested with work slow-downs, working on their own projects in the factory on factory time, and theft (Bruno 1998:5, 11–19; Scott 1990).

In order to find labor discontent in the archaeological record, it is important to develop a thorough contextual analysis of labor conditions. One example is the archaeological analysis performed by Michael Nassaney and Marjorie Abel (1993) at the John Russell Cutlery Company in Turners Falls in the Connecticut River Valley, a leading nineteenth-century knife manufacturer. Established in 1833 in Greenfield, the place is significant because it was one of the first factories to fully mechanize the production of cutlery (Nassaney, McArdle, and Stott 1989:13). Relocated in 1870 to Turners Falls, Massachusetts, it was the largest cutlery factory in the world and a prototype modern cutlery factory (Figure 4.1).

Modernization in the 1880s also came with new management techniques that standardized the production tasks and increased the separations in production. Nassaney and Abel show how discontented workers challenged the existing power structure found in the workplace. Archaeologists discovered a large quantity of artifacts related to interchangeable manufacturing along the riverbank near the former cutting room and trip hammer shop. These objects tended to be inferior or imperfectly manufactured parts from various stages of the production process. While it would be easy to conclude that these artifacts form a typical industrial waste pile, the archaeologists looked at the larger context of nineteenth-century industrial labor relations in which discontented workers often broke machinery, tools, or products. One informant explained that objects were often thrown out of the window and into the river to avoid having to correct manufacturing mistakes (Nassaney, McArdle, and Stott 1989:30–31).

Nassaney and Abel interpret this archaeological signature—the abundance of imperfectly manufactured parts—as a form of defiance against the implementation of the new industrial labor system, which closely regulated their work. Creating and discarding spoiled knives was a form of industrial

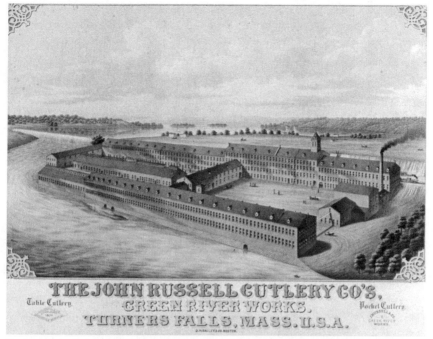

Figure 4.1. Lithograph of the John Russell Cutlery Company's Green River Works, Turners Falls, Massachusetts. Courtesy the Pocumtuck Valley Memorial Association Library.

sabotage and a way to assert some degree of autonomy in the factory (Nassaney and Abel 2000; Saitta 2007:40–41). Their work shows that by understanding context and knowing that discontent existed when manufacturing shifted to the new industrial system, interpretations can be developed related to labor, work, and resistance.

In an international case study at the Eveleigh Railway Workshops in Australia, workers assembled, maintained, and repaired imported and locally manufactured locomotives. In 1917, the managers implemented a form of "scientific management" that became popularized in the United States by Frederick Winslow Taylor. Taylorism timed every movement of the worker. In addition, the factory layout was changed to make for more efficient production and workers were restricted to certain machines. This changed traditional work practices, and in less than two weeks, thirty-three thousand of the forty-eight thousand employees at Eveleigh went on strike to protest. After the strike, the struggles between management and workers continued, although workers successfully found ways to circumvent many of the new restrictions (Taksa 2005:15–22). Taylorism also became widely implemented in industries throughout the United States.

Closer to home, Everett Bassett (1994) shows that early-twentieth-century Apache men participated in the Roosevelt Dam project as wage laborers in an attempt by the federal government to acculturate the Indians to Western norms. However, at the same time, Apache women tended home chores and maintained traditional cultural practices (Bassett 1994). Women played a major role resisting the new capitalist system by maintaining their cultural traditions at the home front.

The study of labor protest camps such as the Ludlow Tent Colony site in Colorado serves as another good example of how archaeologists can explore issues related to labor concerns and living conditions for workers and their families. Through the archaeology of the tent colony, the Ludlow Collective, a multi-institutional group of scholars and students, explored questions about the formation of temporary communities, protest labor movements, and government and military intervention. More important, the archaeology at Ludlow, which is supported by the United Mine Workers of America (UMWA), raises the visibility of this bloody episode in labor relations and is helping to make this incident part of the broader public memory (Ludlow Collective 2001:94–107; McGuire and Reckner 2002:44–58; Walker 2000:60–75; Wood 2002).

In 1903, John D. Rockefeller acquired the Colorado Fuel and Iron Company (CF&I), the largest coal mining, iron ore mining, and steel manufacturing enterprise in the West. About 10 percent of Colorado's population was dependant on CF&I for their livelihood, and in 1913 the company employed fourteen thousand miners, mostly immigrants from southern and eastern Europe (Saitta 2007:45). As one strategy for dealing with the diverse groups working in the mines in 1901, CF&I developed a sociology department to help Americanize and "civilize" the new immigrant. A weekly publication distributed to the workers called *Camp and Plant* helped reinforce corporate policy and the company's work ethic. It contained news about community activities and events and defined proper hygiene, sanitation practices, and morality (Saitta 2007:51)

Despite the company propaganda, the Colorado mines were unsafe and the death rate for miners there was twice the national average; as a result, the miners went on strike for better conditions. The UMWA supported the Ludlow strike and was very concerned about the image of the place and how outsiders would perceive the strikers. The colony consisted of tents with numbers painted on them, all arranged in streets with names and numeri-

Figure 4.2. View of the ruins of Ludlow Tent Colony after the fire. Denver Public Library, Western History Collection, No. Z-199.

cal designations. The strikers placed the doctor's tent at the boarder of the colony, on Front Street. While not as easily accessible as if it was centrally located, it was visible to outsiders, including the press, and conveyed the message that the community was civilized and interested in public health (Saitta 2007:71).

The Ludlow strike ignited a year-long cycle of violence that began in 1913 and culminated when the militia charged the tent colony and set fire to it, killing two women and eleven children. A guerrilla-style war ensued for ten days, and the miners attacked militia encampments, mine guards, and coal mines. The strikers seized control of the mining district in what was called the Ten Days' War (Figure 4.2). The strife at Ludlow is probably one of the best examples of class warfare in American history (Saitta 2007; McGuire and Reckner 2002).

The UMWA soon ran out of funds to support the workers and the strike ended. In the end, the workers received few concessions for their struggle. Some of the official histories written after the strike described the event as being caused by cantankerous Greek and Balkan cultures within the camp rather than highlighting the poor living and working conditions that existed (Saitta 2007).

After the Ludlow Massacre, Rockefeller was ridiculed and demonized by the national press. "In *Harper's Weekly*," Saitta (2007:60–61) notes, "Rockefeller was portrayed as a vulture like creature hovering over the ruins of Ludlow with a caption that read 'Success.'" A commission appointed by President Woodrow Wilson found that Rockefeller was an influential strategist in dealing with the CF&I strike (Saitta 2007:61).

In 1915 Rockefeller toured the strike district, and at the end of his trip he announced that CF&I would create a new labor plan in which workers would have input on conditions that would affect the miners, such as mine safety, health, sanitation, recreation, and education. Known officially as the Employee Representation Plan and informally as the Rockefeller Plan, it gave employees the right to bargain collectively through elected representatives. Houses and living conditions were to be improved, and miners would not lose their jobs if they joined unions (Chernow 1998). Thus while the miners had to abandon their strike, they eventually gained some concessions from CF&I.

George W. Stocking Jr. (1985:116) writes, "While early initiatives in the social sciences ran aground upon the conflict of corporate and philanthropic interest in the aftermath of the 'Ludlow Massacre' in 1914, the elder Rockefeller's creation of the Laura Spelman Rockefeller Memorial in 1918 to further his late wife's social reform interests reopened the possibility of social scientific research." Rockefeller's benevolence was felt throughout the West after Ludlow, in places like Mesa Verde in Colorado, Yellowstone in Wyoming, and Yosemite in California. In 1926, John D. Rockefeller Jr. visited Santa Fe, New Mexico, and asked for a report on the status and needs of the various Santa Fe museums. He showed a special interest in preserving and promoting Indian art and helped support the Indian Arts Fund (Stocking 1981:14; 1982:5). As part of his effort to redeem his image, anthropologists, led by Edgar Lee Hewitt, were successful in establishing the Museum and Laboratory of Anthropology in Santa Fe and received $92,500 in memorial and foundation support over the next ten years.

The archaeology of the Ludlow Tent Colony revealed several tent sites associated with the encamped families. Excavations show that the residents used national brands, which tended to cost more, in the form of canned foods and milk. An analysis of the ceramics from one of the excavated features also indicates that the members of the tent colony did not prescribe to the Victorian era middle-class value of using matched sets of dishes and teawares but only used selected elements of this cultural practice, perhaps a reflection of working-class values (Saitta 2007:76).

Another study related to labor unrest focuses on the bottling works associated with the Harpers Ferry brewery. While monitoring some of the stabilization and rehabilitation of the building, archaeologists found more than one hundred empty beer bottles stashed behind the wall lathing in the former bottling room. They also discovered more than one thousand beer bottles in the basement of the bottling works' elevator shaft, most of them broken after falling more than two stories (Shackel 2000b:104–113).

In the nineteenth century, the typical brewery worker labored about fourteen hours a day, six days per week, and on Sunday for about half this time. By 1910, brewery unions had successfully fought for a ten-hour work day. Workers were exposed to radical temperature shifts and breathed air contaminated with carbonic acid and sulfuric acid, and diseases such as tuberculosis were common. Accidents were almost 30 percent higher in breweries than in other industries because of the higher speeds of the machinery (Hull-Walski and Walski 1994; Schlüter 1910: 255–263). The archaeological evidence suggests that workers drank the owners' profits and concealed their subversive behavior by disposing of otherwise reuseable bottles in walls and by dropping others down the elevator shaft. Fires at the brewery in 1897, 1906, and 1909 coincided with times of labor unrest in the brewery industry, highlighting the link between labor strife and acts of sabotage. Brewing unions eventually made major strides to improve the conditions of the workers (Shackel 2000b:104–113).

In another case study, Jed Levin (1985) compared the archaeological remains of the Telco Block and Supply Company site in New York City and the Supply Mill site in Billerica, Massachusetts (from Schuyler and Mills 1976). He noted that while entrepreneurs increasingly enforced an industrial discipline in the late nineteenth and early twentieth centuries, there was a clear pattern of alcohol use by workers on the job site. Factory work contradicted classical republican ideology, since the wage laborer was at the mercy of the capitalist and the worker could not be an independent citizen (Ross 1985:13). Therefore, skilled workers often resisted the transition to industrial worker and the use of alcohol at these sites may have been a form of resisting work discipline.

Resistance on the Domestic Front

Examining the household domestic assemblages of workers, whose viewpoint regarding work discipline was opposite that of the managers, produced some insight into nearly invisible expressions of social disaffection.

For instance, in the 1840s at the Harpers Ferry armory, laborers and their families readopted old styles of tableware even while both cost and availability made the new and fashionable household goods accessible to the average armory worker family. While some transfer-printed wares were found in the 1840s workers' assemblage, hand-painted wares and creamwares were present at a higher proportion than in the 1820s and 1830s assemblage (Lucas 1994; Lucas and Shackel 1994; for ceramic chronologies, see Miller 1980, 1991; Miller and Hunter 1990; Miller, Martin, and Dickinson 1994). While ceramics became cheaper during the nineteenth century, those who eagerly participated in the armory's industrialization process, such as managers, chose to acquire the new, fashionable goods. Those who rejected the new consumer goods were making choices about what types of goods they should use and purchase (Shackel 1996; also see Miller 1987, 1995; McCracken 1988).

In the domestic sphere, the armory workers' wives were active agents who showed discontent with the new industrial era. While they were probably not protesting the wage labor system, they did protest their role in changing domestic production and their decreasing relations with markets. In this new relationship they were relegated to less control and power overall. They used a material culture that was fashionable generations earlier when they had some control over their everyday lives beyond the domestic sphere. They used these unfashionable goods even though the new consumer material culture was easily accessible and affordable through town merchants. These women did not purchase the same goods as those conforming to liberal republicanism and the ideologies of mass production and mass consumption. They were making choices about what types of goods they should purchase. Here the subtleties of choice among mass-manufactured ceramics are interpreted within the context of explicitly changing political ideologies. The working households chose to reject the new material culture associated with the industrial era and acquired a material culture that was common in their household when they had some control over their means of production (Shackel 1998, 1999b).

Utopian Communities

In some cases, social reformers and charismatic leaders resisted the new culture of capitalism and tried to develop alternative ways of working and living. These movements ran counter to the American ideal of individualism that developed in the early nineteenth century. They developed on the principles of reformed industrialism, improved craft production, or a return to agricultural society. Many people flocked to these communities, although most places lasted only a few years after their organizers moved on or died (Hindle and Lubar 1988:236).

For example, Robert Owen established the New Harmony community in Indiana on the Wabash River in 1825 as a way to develop utopian socialism in an industrial community, a movement that became known as Owenism. He purchased the town from a group of Lutheran Separatists led by George Rapp, who had established the community ten years earlier. Owen had succeeded as an industrialist in England, although he became disenchanted with the affects of industrialization, including the new oppression that developed with industrialization (Boomhower 2002:36; Kamau 1992:69; Williams 1985). In 1796 he served on the Manchester Board of Health and realized that while England had developed tremendous wealth during the industrialization of the textile industry, many more people suffered as a consequence of these economic gains. He believed that mechanization should be used to ease the burden of workers in factories as well as in household activities. In 1800 he purchased the industrial complex at New Lanark, Scotland, where he applied the new technologies and social reform to his textile industrial community (Hindle and Lubar 1988:237). Owen was one of the first industrialists to promote the investment in human capital. While the machine had made slaves of workers, he believed that machinery should be the slave of people. New Lanark is now a UNESCO World Heritage site.

Owen's plan for a socialist community at New Harmony included a town with no more than twenty-five hundred people in which all would work for the common good. It would survive on a mix of small industries and agriculture as an attempt to avoid the ills of urbanization found in industrial centers. All would share the new forms of mechanization, and decisions would get input from the entire community. Owen believed that people were basically good but that the modern industrial environment corrupted people and society. In his opening address at New Harmony on April 27, 1825, Owen explained that he came to the United States to "introduce an entire new State of society; to change it from the ignorant, selfish system, to an enlightened social system, which shall gradually unite all interests into one, and remove all cause for contest between individuals" (Boomhower 2002:37). Owen sank most of his fortune in New Harmony, but he abandoned his effort in 1827 and, while his reform movement continued to grow, returned to England. His efforts had a significant impact in the early industrial era of the United States. About 150 Owenite communities developed throughout the country, most in the Midwest, only to fail in a few years. By 1860, only a handful of Owenite communities survived (Hindle and Lubar 1988:238).

Other utopian communities developed in the form of new religions, such as the Shaker communities, which differed from the Owenite communities in several ways. Founded in 1774 by Mother Ann Lee, a former mill girl from the factories of Manchester, England, Shaker communities believed in celibacy and communal ownership of property. Mechanization was employed to improve handcraft technologies, not factory production. Shaker communities offered an alternative to industrialization as a way to organize the work process. The Shakers developed in New York, and communities were established in New England and the Midwest (Hindle and Lubar 1988:239; Starbuck 1984, 1986; Savulis 1992).

Feltville, New Jersey, established by David Felt, a liberal Unitarian printer and stationer, has also been characterized as a utopian community. It was an early experiment in social engineering and lasted from 1845 to 1860. Matthew Tomaso et al. (2006:33) suggest that Felt established the town at a time when many social thinkers were optimistic about the development of industrial capitalism. The town included a multidenominational church, Felt's factory, a school, and possibly a communal dining room. Felt's summer cottage and house was not significantly larger that the other workers' cottages.

Some Thoughts

Looking at issues of power and the different forms of resistance helps us focus on the impact of industrial capitalism on labor and everyday life. Examining different levels of context shows that the development of this new industrial culture affected not only individuals but also families, communities, and cities. With the onset of industrialism, the rhythms of everyday life changed, as did social relations. A labor archaeology can illuminate how people coped with and resisted the everyday abuses of the industrial system and reveal the different strategies industrialists used to maintain their abusive power (Hardesty 1998; Leone 1984, Saitta 2007; Shackel 2004).

Early documentation exists on strikes, and it shows that there was collective discontent in the industrial process in the United States as early as the 1820s. No doubt other forms of unrecorded resistance, such as work slow-downs and sabotage, existed before, during, and after this time, and with the development of excellent context they can be clearly documented in the archaeological record. Utopian societies also developed as a way to humanize the work process, although many of them failed within a few years of their development.

A labor archaeology should also show how industry changed race, class, and gender relationships. Industry also had an impact on community health and environment, and in many cases health and environment continues to degrade in part due to unchecked capitalism and the continued abuse of the environment. This has lead many concerned citizens to address issues of sustainability. These topics will follow in the next chapter.

5

Directions for a Labor Archaeology

Race and Industry

The relationship between race and industry presents a unique opportunity for those interested in labor archaeology (Shackel 2001; Shackel and Larsen 2000). Industrial slave labor is understudied, and this topic has the potential to not only reveal the inequalities between labor and capital but also highlight the injustices found in race relations in an industrial context.

Through the first half of the nineteenth century, southerners debated over whether industry should be developed in the South. Some argued that the industrial workshops and the horrors of industry should remain north of the Mason-Dixon line, while others wanted to prepare for secession and independence from the North (Hindle and Lubar 1988:203). The first southern cotton mill, established in 1789, hired slaves from the owner of a nearby plantation with the idea that African Americans were well suited to the monotonous and repetitive function of factory work. Mill owners believed that African Americans were a better fit for industry work, which free workers would later call "wage slavery." An 1827 letter in the *American Farmer* (Jones 1989 [1827]:77–79) explained,

> In all extensive manufactories we meet with the veriest dolts, who become, as it were, from habit, adept in the business allotted to them, with a degree of dexterity and precision which appears almost miraculous. . . . Their occupation would be those of mere routine and for this they are peculiarly fitted. . . . The negro possesses, in general, a degree of emulation, equal, at least to that of the white labourers . . . but in my estimation it is superior.

By the middle of the nineteenth century about 5 percent of the enslaved population labored in industrial enterprises as artisans and mechanics (Foner and Lewis 1989:1). Companies owned about 80 percent of the enslaved working in industries, while employers rented the remainder. By

1860, slave states produced almost 25 percent of the country's woolen and cotton textiles (Hindle and Lubar 1988:204).

Antebellum southern iron works employed about ten thousand enslaved workers, and more than thirty thousand worked in sugar refineries, rice mills, grist mills, and textile mills. Some industries employed both white and enslaved blacks in the same factories and mills (Christian 1972; Dew 1966, 1994a, 1994b; Eaton 1961:134–135; Lewis 1979; Miller 1981; Starobin 1970:14–20). Jamie Brandon and James Davidson (2005:113–131) make reference to a form of industrial slavery at the Van Winkle Mill in the Ozark upland South. Jean Libby (1991) provides an extensive review of African American iron workers in western Maryland. However, even with these large numbers of enslaved industrial workers, their presence and contributions are rarely mentioned in the many archaeological reports of these sites. This is partly because archaeologists have largely ignored labor, focusing instead on industrial development. Another reason is that African Americans have not been part of the national story until recently, and their contributions have been overlooked.

Despite the large proportion of African Americans found in various southern industries, in the case of the U.S. Armory at Harpers Ferry, enslaved industrial labor was nonexistent. The armory hired a few enslaved men from their owners and used them in non-industrial occupations, such as laborers, cartmen, and carpenters. They also served as canal lock keepers, plasterers, quarrymen, and stone masons. While the attitude prevailed that African Americans could easily learn the habits of industrialization, they were not trusted to operate the machinery in the gun factory. In fact, various state laws prohibited African Americans from gaining access to firearms (Shackel and Larsen 2000:30–31).

Ann Denkler's (2001:31–32; 2007) research on race in the Shenandoah Valley reveals the importance of the iron industry in relationship to an agricultural community. In particular, the Catherine Furnace and the Shenandoah Iron Works, both dating to 1836, employed enslaved and freed blacks to work in the furnaces along with whites. Today, tourist literature describes the furnaces as important because they supported the Confederacy. Iron from both factories was shipped to Richmond and Harpers Ferry. No sources in the historical society mention the laborers at the site, nor do they recognize the fact that African Americans, freed and enslaved, participated in the industry.

Race and labor relations also become an interesting part of the post–Emancipation era story. After the Civil War, northern industrialists had a chance to hire and train a newly freed work force. Instead, they turned to a new generation of European immigrants, thus shutting out African Americans in many northern industries and keeping many tied to tenant farming in the South (Horton 2000).

In the 1890s, when the official memory of the Civil War began to change, northern industries began their flight to the South in search of cheaper, unorganized labor (Carlton 1982). Until the 1890s, the struggle for emancipation served as one of the official memories of the Civil War, but after the death of Frederick Douglass and the beginning of the Jim Crow era, the emancipationist view of the war lost out to the reconciliationists' memory. Reconciliation developed between white northerners and white southerners, and African Americans and the issues of slavery and the rights of full citizenship for blacks were no longer part of the Civil War story (Blight 2001; Shackel 2003).

Many white southerners experienced a difficult transition into industrial capitalism. They found themselves in an increasingly individualistic and competitive society, and they suffered through the economic recessions of the 1880s and the depression of the 1890s. The move to revitalize a Confederate heritage helped southerners cope with defeat and the imposition of the new industrial order (McConnell 1992:213). While whites worked in the new southern textile industries, African Americans remained disenfranchised. Various forms of corporate paternalism reproduced racial inequalities. An understanding existed whereby African Americans were excluded from manufacturing positions as long as the white work force did not demand too much from their patrons. Racial segregation occurred informally throughout the South, and it was legislated in South Carolina until 1964 (Collins 2002:158). The same is true for industrial sites in the lower middle Atlantic region. In the community of Hampden in northern Baltimore, African Americans were not part of the core of machine operatives. Here, too, an informal agreement existed between the mill owners and the residents to keep blacks out of the mills. The Ku Klux Klan also was active in the neighborhood until the 1990s (Shackel and Gadsby 2008:233).

An overview of the coal-mining industry in Iowa shows that African Americans settled and worked in many coal-mining towns, although they usually were a small minority of the population. A number of Iowa towns did not have any African Americans, and some explicitly excluded them. The Consolidated Coal Company, on the other hand, developed Buxton, Iowa, as a planned town in 1900, and the majority of the townspeople were African Americans who worked in the area's coal mines. The archaeology of Buxton, performed in the early 1980s, examined the material remains of an interracial town that was predominantly inhabited by African Americans in the first quarter of the twentieth century. A minority of the population were of European descent. Whites and blacks worked together, lived next to one another, and shared the same public facilities, although they attended separate churches and voluntary associations (Gradwohl and Osborn 1984:192).

Its former residents remember Buxton largely in idealized terms. In 1909, the *Iowa State Bystander* described it as "the Negro Athens of the north" (Gradwohl 2001). In 1908, the *Southern Workman*, an African American journal published at the Hampden Institute in Virginia, noted that

> the relation [*sic*] of the black majority to the white minority is cordial. . . . The Negroes do not fear the whites and the whites do not try to make them fear them; there is mutual respect. Both races go to school together; the principal and most of the teachers are colored; they go to the same soda-water fountains, ice-cream parlors, and restaurants; work in the same mines, clerk in the same stores, and live side by side. (Wright quoted in Gradwohl 2001:110)

When the company town was disbanded and people resettled in other urban areas, such as Cedar Rapids, Des Moines, Chicago, and Detroit, the former residents of Buxton faced harsh racism in their new communities (Gradwohl 2001:110).

Two field seasons with Iowa State University allowed the Buxton archaeology team to concentrate on three areas in the town. The archaeological remains demonstrated that the residents were part of regional, national, and international trade networks. They also concluded that the spatial layout was a reflection of power and separations. The superintendent's residence, for example, stood on an isolated scenic hilltop across a valley and overlooking the main part of town (Gradwohl and Osborn 1984:192). The project at Buxton helped to bring attention to the study of the archaeology of African Americans in industrial contexts.

While African Americans were disenfranchised from industrial labor in the South, other ethnic groups had to fight prejudices too. For instance, while there was a large migration of Chinese workers to America during the California Gold Rush in the 1850s, they became unwelcome competition for employment by the early 1870s. Embracing social Darwinism, many Anglos considered the new immigrants to be less than human, and anthropologists placed them on the lower end of the evolutionary scale. Chinese immigrants

Figure 5.1. Chinese miners eating and attending to their hair among tents in a California mining camp, 1857. *Harper's Weekly*. Library of Congress, LC-UsZ62-130289.

had few legal rights and could be legally discriminated against. In 1882, the United States legally barred people of Chinese descent from migrating to the United States (Chan 1991; Choy 1995; Orser 2007; Salyer 1995). Chinese work camps are found throughout California and the West, where mineral extraction boomed from the Gold Rush in 1849 through the early twentieth century (Figure 5.1).

In many cases Chinese workers, while facing severe discrimination, maintained strong material and cultural ties to their heritage at the work site and on the domestic front. In one instance, the government prohibited Chinese workers in the Warren Mining District in Idaho until 1869, and only after 1870 were they allowed to lease mining operations. Between 1870 and 1910, five separate Chinese companies mined in the district. Archaeologists found the remains of canvas and repair tools in Warren, indicating that workers constructed impermanent homes in a distinctive Chinese style. Their assemblage contained imported Asian goods such as kitchen utensils and opium bottles, and the workers built Chinese-style garden terraces. Their mining techniques and tools were also different from those of European American miners. The archaeological record shows that the workers at this mining camp retained their strong Chinese heritage on the domestic front as a result of, rather than in spite of, discrimination (Elliott 1994; Striker and Sprague 1993).

Barbara Voss (2005) reminds us that we need to be careful about creating oppositions and developing heritage for any ethnic group with the idea that the archaeological assemblages are a product of a static community with a fixed identity. In fact, efforts to identify differences in the material culture used in everyday behavior to define group boundaries have often proved challenging. While many archaeologists have created oppositions to highlight differences between overseas Chinese and Western cultures, there are also many cultural remains that are similar to other non-Chinese sites. She notes Sherri Gust's work, which shows how the faunal assemblages varied between overseas Chinese households. Gust (1993:208) observed that the butchering marks found in the remains of some of the households indicated a "standard Euroamerican style" of food preparation. R. Scott Baxter and Rebecca Allen (2002:292–296) also show that the San Jose, California, Chinese community had many economic ties to American manufacturers and distributors, thus potentially blurring any forms of easily identifiable cultural markers.

Gender and the Industrial Era

The development of wage labor dramatically changed the family structure and gender relations. The integrated family economy quickly faded and the division of gender roles became explicit in urban areas during the early nineteenth century. Industrialization affected the home and the workplace at the same rate, although the experiences in both were quite different (Cowan 1983). While society industrialized, labor reorganized and new technologies replaced older ones in the household. Boydston (1990:101) notes, "What is most striking about the early industrial period is, not how different housework was becoming from paid labor, but rather how closely the reorganization of the two forms of work was replicating each other." The changes in the household were directly linked to the changes in modern society. As the rest of the industrializing world became engulfed with time consciousness, the household also operated within those constraints. Meals had to be served at specific times to accommodate family members whose schedules were dictated by machines and work shifts. Harriet Beecher Stowe wrote that the wife had become the very embodiment of time and family (Boydston 1990:104–105).

In the early nineteenth century, middle-class women were in charge of refinement within the home, and they became responsible for promoting their home among friends and acquaintances (Wall 1994:147–158). Women also were involved in the ritualization process of the meal. The creation of specific times for meals helped to ritualize middle-class life, and as women increasingly influenced the domestic sphere, their role in this ritualization also increased dramatically (Wall 1994:111). When held on a regular and timely basis, and when all family members participated, the ritual of the family meal taught "punctuality, order, neatness, temperance, self-denial, kindness, generosity, and hospitality" (Sedgwick, quoted in Wall 1994:112). As Diana Wall (1994:147) notes, the "sensory stimulus of the food was the primary focus of family... meals. ... The dishes simply provided a frame for the important item, the food itself." During the nineteenth century, middle-class urban women began to ritualize family meals and the dishes became a vehicle to present the meal. They were physical symbols manipulated as part of the ritual.

By the 1820s, middle-class women were helping to further institutionalize the meal's ritualization. Serving courses became more specialized at this time, and the number of courses increased. As a result, the number of dishes used in each meal increased (Wall 1994). Lu Ann DeCunzo (1995:140–141) notes the importance of various uses for different sets of dinner wares. She explains that an 1828 etiquette book noted that a proper household needed to have three sets of dinner services, one for company, one for ordinary use, and the third for the kitchen servants.

Wall (1994:160–162) compares the ceramic assemblages from lower-middle-class and upper-middle-class families in mid-nineteenth-century New York City. In both groups, women created their domestic worlds. Both had tablewares and teawares, although the wealthier family had more than one set. For instance, the wealthier household owned one porcelain and one ironstone tea set, while the poorer household owned only one ironstone tea set. The wealthier household subscribed to the rules of etiquette, while the poorer household did not have porcelain goods for display.

Little (1997:231) asks, Does the lack of competitive display shows rejection of competition in favor of friendly cooperation? Or does it suggest withdrawal from the competitive arena in the face of hopelessness? Is withdrawal analogous to resistance? Are subcultures' alternative, muted cultural expressions necessary to the dominant culture's dominance? While the home was perceived as a "refuge from sadness," it was also a place where people played out their responses to the social pressures of the time.

In her study, Margaret Wood (2004) focuses on the southern Colorado coal town of Berwind, which was established in 1892 and abandoned in 1931. She argues that household relations are not necessarily isolated from society or the broader political and social relationships that are part of the public domain. By placing women in the center of her discussion, she shows how they were instrumental in class action and in resisting capitalist oppression. The households at Berwind did not necessarily conform to middle-class expectations for domesticity but created a world that served their middle-class needs. Many of the coal miners lived in conditions of poverty and oppression. To combat this poverty, after the turn of the century women increasingly took in boarders. In the beginning of the decade, 14 percent of households had boarders, but at the end of the decade that number had increased to 45 percent. An examination of the archaeological record shows a significant increase in the amount of mass-produced canned goods found in these later assemblages. Prior to World War I, the cost of canned beef could be as much as 100 percent more than fresh beef, and canned beans could be 30 to 40 percent higher than fresh beans. The additional income to the family created by women caring for boarders allowed families to purchase food that was considered healthy, nutritious, and a luxury (Wood 2004:225). While this mining community had families representing more than two dozen nationalities, women built ties between families of different ethnic origins. In one case study, Wood documents how women of different ethnic backgrounds helped one another with child care, childbearing, and some forms of housework. They also shared coffee (rather than the expected and middle-class tea), which helped build relations between groups.

Environment, Health, and Industry

Labor archaeology also can examine issues related to health conditions at industrial sites and towns and provide us with examples of sustainability. For instance, many mining sites endangered the health and life of workers. Work sites were often unstable, machinery often malfunctioned, pollution and harmful fumes contaminated the air, and workers often put in long and exhausting hours. All of these variables led to accidents, chronic illnesses, and deaths. Industrialists were known for their efforts to accelerate their machinery, which in turn led to increased fatigue and an amplified rate of injuries for workers (Schivelbusch 1986). At the Russell Cutlery factory there is good evidence of other dangers, such as shattered grind stones that were reported to have knocked workers unconscious. Additionally, silica dust, a byproduct of manufacturing knives, would have inflamed and scarred worker's lungs (Nassaney, McArdle, and Stott 1989).

Industry often grew at the expense of the environment. For instance, in mining districts ore contains valuable mineral deposits that can be mined and extracted through various processing techniques. Because of the cycles of supply and demand and the relative cost of extracting minerals, the price of copper, for example, can be high enough that ore containing less that 0.05 percent metal can be profitable. As a result, waste piles of ore are abundant throughout some mining landscapes. Coal mixed with rock waste, known as culm, from anthracite mines are also plentiful in mining districts (Gordon and Malone 1994:44–45).

Another environmental hazard is the many underground fires that exist in the abandoned coal mines. For instance, in 1962 in Centralia, Pennsylvania, residents started a fire when they burned trash in an abandoned strip mine that was connected to underground workings. Today the fire is still burning and spreading, releasing smoke and fumes, forcing residents to abandon their homes as the ground warms, and destroying vegetation in its vicinity (Gordon and Malone 1994:125). The town had one thousand residents in 1981, but by 2000 there were only about twenty-one people remaining. There are no plans to extinguish the fire, which is consuming an eight-mile seam containing enough coal to fuel the fire for 250 years. This phenomenon is not uncommon. China, one of the world's fastest industrializing nations, has more than fifty coal fires that may burn for centuries (Krajick 2005:52–61).

Industrialists paid little attention to the impact that factories had on the surrounding environment until workers, scientists, and environmentalists brought these issues to the forefront of the American consciousness in the mid-twentieth century. One well-known example of the impact of environmental stress and pollution on the health of a working community comes from Donora, a town along the Monongahela River in Pennsylvania. Incorporated in 1901, the town contained coke ovens, coal stoves, zinc furnaces, metal works, and steel mills. The shrieking mill whistles guided the daily routines of its citizens (Davis 2002a:6). Fumes from the town's industrial plants became part of the everyday environment. The landscape stood mostly barren of vegetation because of these poisonous gases (Davis 2002b:B9). Oral accounts attest to the town's extreme pollution as women reminisced about washing their curtains every week. And by the time the women had washed the last window in a house, the first one was dirty again. It was common to see elderly people in town with oxygen tanks. One person

Figure 5.2. Wire mill spewing smoke along the Monongahela River, Donora, Pennsylvania, c. 1910. Library of Congress, LC-USZ62-131258.

remarked, "Well, we used to say, 'That's not coal dust, that's gold dust.' As long as the mills were working, the town was in business. That's what kept your Zadde and your father employed. Nobody was going to ask if it made a few people ill. People had to eat" (Davies 2002a:8) (Figure 5.2). Donora's death rate was significantly higher than the death rates in the surrounding nonindustrial towns.

Donora became infamous on October 26, 1948, when a massive blinding smog covered the town. A temperature inversion over the entire Monongahela Valley trapped the smoke and fumes of the steel mills and zinc furnace. The fumes became so thick that traffic stopped along the town's roads because of reduced visibility. The noxious poisonous gases killed twenty-four people in twenty-four hours. The steelworkers union sponsored an investigative study into the sudden deaths of the workers and townspeople of Donora. Only partial and preliminary reports exist, and what scant information exists shows that those who died had twelve to twenty-five times the normal level of fluoride in their blood, a clear case of fluoride poisoning. While the investigative team never produced a final report, and the source of poison was never officially identified, the incident at Donora made the country more aware of the impact that a polluted environment can have on human health (Davis 2002a: 15–25).

Mrozowski (2006:150) points out that while late-nineteenth-century society began to recognize the relationship between poor sanitation and health problems, lead poisoning remained unnoticed. Soil samples from the boardinghouse, tenement, and the overseers' block at Lowell, Massachusetts, all produced high levels of lead in the soil. The archaeological contexts were sealed, so there was little modern contamination. Lead-based paints and deteriorating lead plumbing contributed to this high level. While children from Lowell's factories faced class and ethnic discrimination, they also suffered from lead poisoning, which probably led to poor performance in school and the stereotyping of this student group.

In a study of human osteological remains comparing medieval urban and early industrial sites in England, Lewis (2002) shows the devastating impact of industrialization on children. Children from industrial towns showed a higher rate of mortality, retarded growth, higher levels of stress, and a greater prevalence of metabolic and infectious diseases. Children from an industrial town were also more than an inch shorter than those from a contemporary urban trading town. While differences in urban and rural populations existed in the past, Lewis (2002:211–223) argues that industrialization had the greatest impact on child health.

Archeologists have demonstrated the effectiveness of using soil samples from the area in and around factories and dwellings to search for toxins to examine general health conditions. Privy samples at workplaces may reveal the presence of parasites and other toxins, indicating the health level in a community (Reinhard 1994; Reinhard, Mrozowski, and Orloski 1986; Beaudry, Cook, and Mrozowski 1991). Exploring general sanitation landscape features (Ford 1994) and identifying the presence of medicinal and alcohol bottles may also provide clues regarding workers' general health (Bond 1989; Larsen 1994). Industrial pollution has had a devastating impact on humans and the natural environment, and it is important that these issues of sustainability are made part of the story of industry and labor.

Some Thoughts

Earlier in this book I suggested that in order to become relevant to a larger public audience, archaeology needs to address questions that are pertinent to contemporary society. Housing and the built environment are important issues that affect our everyday lives. This chapter connects archaeology and industrial society to race, gender, the natural environment, and issues related to general health. While race and gender studies are not new to historical archaeology, they are important issues that are relevant to and affect local communities and society as a whole. In addition, as we increasingly pay attention to issues such as global warming and the poisoning of the environment, archaeology can make the connection between the past and the present and provide important examples about how to treat our environment and how the impact of pollution and poisons unequally affect those who do not have the resources to protect themselves and avoid these hazardous conditions. As the American public grows more concerned with the issue of sustainability, archaeology can provide excellent case studies about the consequences of unchecked capitalism and the impact on the environment and human health.

6

Memory, Ruins, and Commemoration

As the labor movement has been weakened significantly over the past few decades, representing labor in the official memory has not come easily. Labor often competes with capital when creating a memory of the industrial past. The power of capital frequently wins out over local labor groups when communities debate on how to remember industry on the landscape. Understanding how and why some groups tend to remember a particular past while others forget or ignore a past is an important issue for critically evaluating and understanding how labor and industry are represented on the landscape.

For instance, at Saugus Iron Works the theme of industrial progress takes precedence over the story of labor. The iron works developed in 1647 near the head of the Saugus River in Massachusetts, east of Boston. Since the iron works were not profitable, after 1652 it operated on a part-time basis. Twenty-four years later its owners abandoned the operations (Gordon and Malone 1994).

The late 1940s and early 1950s archaeology of Saugus by Roland W. Robbins provided the groundwork for many of the reconstructions found at Saugus today. The excavations uncovered a holding pond and canal, a wheel pit, and half of a blast-furnace waterwheel, along with thousands of iron-works artifacts. While overshot, undershot, and pitchback wheels are used in the modern-day reconstruction of the iron works, only the overshot wheel at the blast furnace is faithfully reconstructed based on the archaeology. The other reconstructions often followed contemporary European works and in several cases ignored archaeological evidence. In the midst of the reconstructions at Saugus, the only visible sign that remains from the seventeenth-century landscape is a ridge formed by the accumulation of slag that extends to the river (Linebaugh 2000:11–18; 2005:61–80). Archaeology done at the iron works is an example of Americans searching for emblems of industrial prowess during the early Cold War era. The archaeology and reconstructions help provide a continuum of three hundred years of industrial knowledge in the United States. When the site was restored, a

Figure 6.1. Reconstruction at the Saugus Iron Works National Historic Site, 1998. Photograph by Paul A. Shackel.

self-guided tour brochure titled *Welcome to the Saugus Iron Works Restoration: Birthplace of America's Iron and Steel Industry, Saugus, Mass.* was created for visitors (Carlson 1991:38). The iron works is now part of the Saugus Iron Works National Historical Site, and the commemoration of this site places early industrial enterprise in the consciousness of Americans (Figure 6.1). Nevertheless, exhibits at the site do not promote the histories of the workers and their living conditions at the iron works.

In the 1970s, the United States was entering its postindustrial age and industrialists began abandoning factories at a rapid rate. Sociologist John Urry (1990:107) explains this phenomenon:

> The remarkably rapid de-industrialization . . . in the late 1970s and the early 1980s has two important effects. On the one hand, it created a profound sense of loss, both of certain kinds of technology . . . and of the social life that had developed around those technologies. . . . One the other hand, much of this industry had historically been based in inner-city . . . premises, large numbers of which became available for alternative uses.

In some instances, monumental landscapes, memorials, and museums developed to remember the industrial prowess of a fading era. In the many former industrial sites that have become regional and national museums, visitors are often told about the glories of economic and social progress as a result of industrial achievements. The federal government has helped in supporting the commemoration of industrial capitalism by creating "sacred" places such as Saugus National Historic Site (1968), Springfield Armory National Historic Site (1978), Lowell National Historical Park (1978), and the Blackstone River Valley National Heritage Corridor (1986). At many of these places the past is being used to celebrate the benefits of industrial capitalism. In other places, communities are debating about what to do with these ruins and, if saved, how to portray them to the public.

England's well-preserved medieval ruins are an example of how a society uses structural remains on the landscape to remember its past. The ideal of the ruin in literature and painting came out of the romantic era, which developed during the late eighteenth century as a reaction to Enlightenment ideals and the industrial revolution. Romanticism placed new emphasis on such emotions as trepidation, horror, and the experience of confronting untamed nature (Nottingham Castle Museum 1988). The increased appreciation of nature and of medieval ruins in nature were represented in various forms of art, from oil paintings and engravings to scenes drawn on ceramic vessels. Ideally, these representations included interplay between dark and light, trees and rambling shrubs, and a few figures, either human or animal. Viewing the ruins produced a mix of emotions for experiencing the landscape (Edensor 2005; Janowitz 1990).

Ruins came to be viewed as part of a cycle of life and death, and they represented the idea that all humans and the built environment would return to this inevitable state of ruin and/or decay. The depopulation of the rural landscape for larger cities, leaving abbeys, castles, and farmsteads in a state of decay, seemed to mock the optimism of the new industrial order. While industrialists were making claims of progress, the landscape was scattered with decaying ruins that foreshadowed the inevitability of death and decay of the new industrial order. Ruins meant imminent degeneration and collapse (Edensor 2005:11–12).

The "cult of ruins" became so profound in the late eighteenth and early nineteenth centuries that wealthy estate owners created ruins on their estates. They served as a tangible reminder of the impermanence of stone, brick, mortar, and flesh. They also served as a way to present a landscape with a long tradition of heritage (Janowitz 1990:2).

In a similar fashion, industrial ruins can be used to show a long presence of industrial might in a region or country. Tim Edensor (2005:7) contests the notion that industrial "ruins are spaces of waste, that contain nothing, or nothing of value, and that they are saturated with negativity as spaces of danger, delinquency, ugliness and disorder." Rather, he states, they signify an area's former prosperity and its uncertain future. Ruins posses a rich history that is often forgotten in the rubble and decay. However, when we preserve a ruin, "we reclaim that object from its fall into decay and oblivion and often for some kind of cultural attention and care that, in a sense, elevates its value. In the European traditions the classical ruin is elevated out of oblivion into a particularly exalted position of contemplation or even worship" (Roth 1997:1).

Harpers Ferry serves as an example of a place where the preservation of ruins occurred at a relatively early stage in the history of the United States. After the Civil War, many of the buildings at Harpers Ferry stood in ruins, and the industrial ruins, such as the U.S. Armory buildings and Herr's flour mill, became part of an intentionally memorializing landscape. The landscape commemorated the once economically prosperous regional manufacturing center. The ruins created a new commemorative landscape, and townspeople, industrialists, and the Baltimore and Ohio Railroad went to great lengths to preserve these ruins and transform the area from a manufacturing town to a symbol of industrial precedence. By the early twentieth century, the armory buildings had disappeared from the landscape; however, the railroad outlined the buildings' foundations. The industrial ruins functioned as a conduit to the past by creating monuments to the early industrial era. The commemoration at Harpers Ferry (as well as in other areas throughout the country) helped reinforce an industrial consciousness and still serves as a reminder of the "immutable" traditions of industrialization (Shackel 1994) (Figure 6.2). As National Park Service historian Richard Sellars (1987:19) notes, "Even without monuments, [preservation] is an act of memorializing. Preservation acknowledges that something so important happened that it must be remembered and at least some terrain set aside." Allowing ruins to stand in a decaying state is a form of preservation that memorializes past events.

Preservation, reuse, and demolition are all under consideration by communities as old industrial centers try to revitalize and again become economically viable (Holt 2006). Industrial ruins can be a good touchstone for remembering working-class history, and that may be a reason why some city governments and investors wish to have them disappear from the landscape. Several decades ago Leary (1979) suggested that the restoration of nineteenth-century factories could be useful in interpreting and understanding industrial work conditions. Telling the story of labor's struggle

Figure 6.2. Outline of armory ruins at Harpers Ferry, West Virginia, in the early twentieth century. Courtesy Harpers Ferry National Historical Park.

can make the preservation of industrial complexes more acceptable to a greater portion of the working-class community. Industrial archaeology has the potential to be an educational tool that provides "a sort of Rosetta Stone to decipher the language peculiar to industrial tombs" (Leary 1979:182).

As the United States deindustrializes and steel factories and textile mills fade into the historical consciousness, the history of the places are softened and the day-to-day anxieties that developed between labor and capital often fade into the shadows of the place. These histories are often sanitized and romanticized and become redefined as heritage (Lowenthal 1996; Walker 1999). Some members of the working class view the preservation of old buildings and ruins as an attempt to save a degrading phase of human history. Robert Vogel once noted that the "dirt, noise, bad smell, hard labor and other forms of exploitation associated with these kinds of places make preservation [of industrial sites] ludicrous. 'Preserve a steel mill?' people say, 'It killed my father. Who wants to preserve that?'" (Lowenthal 1985:403). Mary Blewett (1979) also writes about the demolition of many of Lowell's boardinghouses on Dutton Street as "working class revenge." In 1966, the city's working-class residents and officials did battle with preservationists who wanted to save the buildings and glorify the paternalistic era of Lowell's history. A city councilor argued that the boardinghouses were "a part of our history that should be forgotten" (Ryan 1989:82). Therefore, when thinking about remembering industrial sites, or in fact any place, it is important to recognize that individual, dissenting views may differ with preservationists' goals. Archaeology can help develop a better understanding of life and work in an industrial capitalist system, although the discipline still has a long way to go to meet Leary's (1979) expectations.

Michael Shanks and Randall McGuire (1996) remind us that the act of archaeology is a form of commemoration, and when we do archaeology we create a memory of the past that is rooted in our present-day concerns. Therefore, labor archaeology can be a way to remember and unveil a history that has been buried all too long. Faced with deteriorating conditions, labor organized in order to protect workers' rights as citizens, ensuring that they would get a decent wage to support themselves and their families. An archaeology that emphasizes these issues can only help to remember and commemorate these histories.

However, when citizens and scholars try to present new and different interpretations that challenge the consensus history, they often are confronted by those who demand the status quo. The media occasionally portrays revisionist histories as unpatriotic, antigovernment, and anti-American, and scholars are seen as left-wing radicals who are overly concerned with "political correctness," ignoring the real point of revisionist history—understanding a multivocal past. Mark Leff (1995:843) remarks:

> This epithet, "revisionist," . . . may be the key to understanding the current crisis of history. "Revisionist" meant the displacement of the more happy-faced, elite oriented view of American progress and destiny to which most Americans, particularly those raised on "consensus history" textbooks, had become accustomed. At the same time, the use of "revisionist" as a term of abuse suggests a rejection of the very notion of historical reinterpretation, under the assumption that the displaced version of history had been objective and factual, while revisions were subjective and faddish.

Celebrating labor's heritage has never been part of the mainstream history in the United States because it confronts capital and is therefore seen as revisionist. Labor's heritage is about the struggle for better working conditions, and these histories are important to workers today (Saitta 2007). Whether victories or defeats, it is important for the labor movement to remember the struggles and learn from past efforts.

James Green (2000:151) notes that working in the industrial South often meant an early death, since there were few unions that insisted on workplace safety protection. And to this date the general public remains unaware of the horrific workplace conditions of America's past, except for the occasional headline that exposed the consequences of unregulated working environments.

Sometimes, commemorating those who died in industrial accidents is difficult because their final resting places are difficult to find. The Mount Calvert Cemetery in McAlester, Oklahoma, is one of the few places of commemoration. Here, there is a mass grave containing the remains of thirty-two Mexican immigrant miners who died in a gas explosion in 1929. Will Rogers led a national campaign to raise money for this gravesite, and the Mexican government contributed funds. A single wooden cross marks the site (Green 2000:151–152).

Another place of commemoration is the gravesite of Martin Irons, who led a strike against the Southern Pacific Railroad in 1886. After the event, Irons was blacklisted, but he continued to speak out for organized labor and against monopolies and their influence on government. He died in 1900 in Texas, and a monument was erected on his grave 1911, when working-class people were part of a powerful movement that resisted exploitation. They saw the Southern Pacific's owner as hateful because he boasted that he could "hire one half of the working class to kill the other half" (Green 2000:152). The Irons monument was built in a cooperative effort between the Knights of Labor and the People's Party, and the Texas State Federation of Labor was officially in attendance during its dedication.

In other cases, the testimony of defeated strikers often has been repressed, and indeed it continues to be muted. The story of the labor strife at Lawrence, Massachusetts, only surfaced and became part of the community's identity in the late 1970s. The story of the massive textile strike of southern workers in 1934 was repressed for many decades. In the beginning of the Great Depression, President Roosevelt's National Industrial Recovery Act promised a northern standard of wages and hours for all industrial workers. Employers refused to abide by the law and mill workers went on strike throughout the South and in parts of the Northeast. The "uprising of '34" surprised most of the southern elite. They expected loyalty from their workers, since under their paternalistic control poor whites were enabled to work at the exclusion of blacks. "Poor white mill hands," Green (2000:160) notes, "lived in tightly controlled company towns, accepted the benefits of corporate paternalism, worshiped in conservative Protestant churches, and shared a southern regional identity with their employers presumably based on white supremacy, Victorian morality, and hostility to Yankees, especially to labor organizations."

The National Guard responded in some places, and seven strikers were killed in Honea Path, South Carolina. Green (2000:161) believes that the strike revealed antagonisms that traditionally had been silenced. Ten thousand people marched in mourning for the dead, but the victims were soon forgotten in the collective memory. The memory of the strike and the killing appeared to be suppressed by the community. The strikers were either discouraged by their defeat or believed that the events would some day come back to haunt them. The strike created divisions in communities, and some churches would not allow the dead strikers to be buried in church cemeteries. The memory was suppressed until the Southern Oral History Program began interviewing textile workers and filmmakers began creating a documentary of the event. Green (2000:161) notes that "*The Uprising of '34* was shown on public television all over the nation on Labor Day 1996, except in South Carolina, one of those places where a kind of conspiracy developed to hide a bloody secret involving class warfare."

In the 1980s and 1990s, working communities continued to see the loss of industrial jobs, and jobs with benefits were replaced with part-time and contractual jobs. Capital continued to hold the upper hand as communities were affected by the increased mobilization of firms. Burrows (quoted in Collins 2002:154) suggests that the "tyranny of the overseer over individual workers has been replaced by the tyranny of capital mobility over the collective worker. . . . The fear of being fired is replaced by the fear of capital flight, plant closure, transfer of operations and plant disinvestments." This trend means less bargaining power for workers, including fewer pay raises, the loss of benefits, and reduced health and safety measures at work. The tie between employer and community has diminished significantly, and in many cases the corporate investment in the community has ceased or diminished significantly (Collins 2002:155).

At Ludlow, more than twelve thousand workers went on strike for better wages and working conditions in September 1913. April of the following year marked one of the bloodiest assaults on American organized labor. In an armed conflict with the National Guard, twenty-six people were killed, including a dozen women and children. The UMWA proposed the erection of a monument memorializing the incident in 1916, and it was completed two years later. It commemorates the workers who died in the massacre, depicting a miner along with a woman embracing a child. The "Death Pit," where the women and children were killed, was preserved in concrete. The place has become a memorial as well as a rallying place for workers. "They were striking for the work benefits we enjoy today," Dean Saitta, one of the project's co-principals, remarked. "Safe working conditions, the eight-hour workday—these are things that the strikers were lobbying for. If we value those workplace benefits, it's good to remind ourselves every now and then that they were won with blood and gained through struggle" (*University of Denver Magazine* 2003).

The meaning and memory of Ludlow are not necessarily unified and sanitized in the local and public memory of the place. When John L. Lewis took control of the UMWA in the 1910s, many of the Ludlow strike leaders formed a separate union in southern Colorado. By purchasing the land around the Ludlow Massacre, the UMWA made it clear that the place belonged to all miners, not just those who worked in the area. In 1927, when the International Workers of the World (IWW) went on strike and used Ludlow as a rallying point, the UMWA leadership became outraged because the IWW made a connection between their struggle and the Ludlow incident (Walker 1999).

Saitta (2007:46) describes how labor commemoration can sometimes be misunderstood. The Ludlow Tent Colony, a place where women and children were killed during the 1913–14 coal strike, is marked by a memorial. If you acquire a road map from the American Automobile Association or at a tourist information station along a Colorado highway, the place is marked "Ludlow Massacre site." While doing archaeology, the project conducted a survey of the tourists who came by and nearly 60 percent of those who filled out the questionnaire said that they thought the place was the site of an Indian massacre. Few people expected a monument to American labor wars. Organized labor in the West does not seem to be part of people's perceptions of the region. Rather, people tend to have a romantic idea of the free, wandering cowboy in the West, when in fact they, like industrial laborers, were tied into the larger capitalist system. Cowboys, too, sometimes took action to transform their economic relations by going on strike. For instance, the

Figure 6.3. The memorial at Ludlow, Colorado, commemorating the men, women, and children killed in the Ludlow Massacre in 1914. Photograph by Paul A. Shackel, 2007.

Cowboy Strike of 1883 saw several hundred cowboys walk off their jobs at five major Texas ranches for better pay (McGuire and Reckner 2002:46).

I visited the site in the summer of 2007 and found an array of stickers from various local unions paying homage to those who fell at Ludlow. The meaning of this monument has not gone uncontested. In 2003, an unknown vandal decapitated the head of the statue, but in 2005 the monument was restored and rededicated by the UMWA (*Militant* 2005). A fence surrounds the statue. Working people still struggle for basic rights, and Ludlow is often the rallying point for their concerns and serves as one of the best examples of class warfare in the United States (McGuire and Reckner 2002) (Figure 6.3).

Another example of the struggle to control the memory of a labor strike is Haymarket in Chicago. In 1886, industrial workers protested for an eight-hour work day, and workers at the McCormick factory went on strike to support this measure. On May 4 about three thousand people heard speeches from anarchists and socialists decrying the murders of strikers who had been killed the previous day. At the end of the day the event turned violent. As the protest was ending, about two hundred police officers marched on the dwindling crowd and ordered them to disperse. A bomb was thrown into the police formation and the police retaliated by firing on the protesters. Four demonstrators were killed and many injured. Seven officers died and another sixty were injured, many from cross-fire. Eight of the strike leaders were arrested and all were convicted; seven were sentenced to death and one to prison. Four of the seven who were sentenced to death were hanged on May 11, 1887. Two had their sentences commuted to life in prison by the governor, and one hanged himself the morning of the execution. Civic authorities banned those executed from being buried inside the city of Chicago, thereby forcing the labor union to bury them in Waldheim Cemetery in Forest Park, outside of the city limits (Foote 1997:133–140).

The Haymarket memorialization became a struggle between competing interests (Dabakis 1998). The business community claimed the police were martyrs and proclaimed that they were "Protectors of Chicago," even though the police had helped ignite the riot. Business leaders claimed the site of the bombing, erected a monument to the police in 1888, and prevented labor from memorializing its martyrs within the city limits. The martyrs' gravesite at Waldheim Cemetery became the commemorative place for industrial workers. A large memorial, depicting justice in the figure of a woman placing a laurel wreath on the head of a fallen worker with her left hand and holding a drawn sword in the other hand, marks the grave. Thousands came to its unveiling in 1893, and it remains a pilgrimage site and a subject of regular commemoration (Foote 1997:136–137).

A tension remained between the police and labor and anarchists into the late twentieth century. However, in the early twenty-first century, funding from the Illinois state legislature became available for a commemorative park dedicated to the right for free speech. In order to create some sort of reconciliation between labor and the police, a panel consisting of representatives from the Chicago Police Department and the Illinois Labor History Society was convened. Together, along with representatives from other city organizations, they planned a common memorial at the Haymarket site. Reconciliation is especially important to the police because they

Figure 6.4. The 2004 monument erected at Haymarket in Chicago. Photograph by
Paul A. Shackel, 2007.

are now unionized and part of organized labor. Yet it is unclear—in fact, it
is doubtful—that the opinions of anarchists and their views on and critique
of capitalism and industry were solicited, even though it was the anarchists
who led the strike at Haymarket (Kelland 2005:36).

The cooperation between the police and labor, these once confronta-
tional groups, was remarkable, reaching a consensus on how to remember
the Haymarket events. The president of the Chicago Fraternal Order of Police stated, "We are part of the labor movement now and glad to be there"
(Kelland 2005:36). The monument, erected in 2004, depicts workers constructing a wagon, and an anonymous figure is on the platform, a symbol of
the platform on which the workers gave speeches on the day of the riot. The
statue conveys a message of free assembly and free speech, something that
is palpable for all involved in the project. The labor of anonymous agents
as well as labor as a whole are represented in the memorial, but the monument does not represent the martyrs or any of the subjects of the event. The
radical social critique of government and industry is clearly absent from
this new public display at Haymarket. Clearly, the changing meaning of the
place, imposed by a new partnership, has led some to criticize it as a heritage
of newfound "safeness" (Figure 6.4).

Some Thoughts

What is studied and remembered at industrial sites shows us who we are as a community of scholars and citizens of a nation. Often there are inconsistencies between the official and unofficial memories at industrial sites. The memory of industry and its representation on the American landscape is like the memory of all significant events in history. There are winners and losers. Representing labor on the American landscape can help us focus on an important aspect of our American heritage—the hard-won rights of workers to acquire better work conditions and a decent standard of living.

Conclusion

This book has focused on the American experience and its relationship to the development of industry and working-class life. While the "new labor history" was formalized in the 1970s (Brody 1979, 1980, 1989, 1993; Dubofsky 2000:21; Gutman 1976; Montgomery 1979; Wallace 1978), its foundation existed in the late nineteenth century. During the Progressive era, politicians, reformers, trade unionists, and labor radicals as well as social scientists turned their attention to the "labor problem" or the "labor question" (Smith 1991:570). Scholars wrote about the struggle between labor and capital and the substandard living and working conditions of working-class families (Fitzpatrick 1991:423). Intellectuals such as Richard Ely endorsed the labor movement and tied their mission to the progress of labor and the advancement of reform (Fitzpatrick 1991:423; Fink 1991:396–399). In the early twentieth century, others, such as Edith Abbott, believed that unskilled and unorganized labor should also be the focus of labor history and that that history should include African Americans, immigrants, children, and female workers (Fitzpatrick 1991:427).

The growth of industry after the American Civil War had a tremendous impact on workers and their families. From the early nineteenth through the early twentieth centuries, industrial salaries generally decreased while the geographical mobility of workers increased significantly. The development of new transportation systems lowered the cost of the movement of products and lessened the importance of geography (Hiscox 2002:404). The development of labor-saving machinery and the introduction of the production line also encouraged the use of unskilled workers. Children were a prime source of unskilled labor. Cunningham's (2000) study of child labor shows how cultures differed in their attitudes toward employing children. In early twentieth-century Japan, for example, children did not work, whereas in Belgium children were at times worked to death (Gratton and Moen 2004:364–365).

The Progressives blamed the high number of children working in U.S. factories on the "peasants" from southern Europe, who, they said, did not know civilized American culture. In one published study a group of immigrant Italian men were interviewed in 1919. They reported that as young men they were bonded to work for two to three years and they expected their children to do the same (Gratton and Moen 2004). Child labor supplemented the family's income, although industrialists paid children a fraction of what adult males earned. In the United States, reformers supported the idea that children should be nurtured, protected, and shielded from the workplace. They felt that children should be in schools to be educated and to learn to be Americans (Gratton and Moen 2004:356–358). Rebecca Yamin's (2002) archaeological analysis of the Five Points area of New York City proposes that finding children's toys in this working-class neighborhood suggests that at least some families encouraged children to be children rather than having them labor in factories. Some families were able to resist placing their children in the labor market, at least for a part of their preadolescent years.

The period between 1910 and 1930 marks the beginning of a general increase in salaries among industrial workers and a decrease in worker mobility. Industrial jobs became increasingly skilled and industrialists encouraged workers to stay at their job longer with higher salaries and other benefits. This trend continued into the late twentieth century (Hiscox 2002:406). In the United States, the rate of child labor fell from the beginning of the twentieth century. The introduction of child labor laws coincided with the increase in wages and skills needed for industrial work in order to operate in a more complex industrial environment (Basu 1999).

Progressive era reformers also wrote about the chaotic, unnatural, and unsanitary living conditions that had a severe impact on the urban industrial worker (Figure C.1). Solutions ranged from radical socialist revolutions to more conservative approaches that slightly modified capitalism. These reforms, which became widely adopted, included providing more affordable services to workers, such as the municipalization of electricity, sewage, and water systems. Well-planned living environments, they believed, would make better citizens and better workers because workers would feel gratitude for the industrialist who made these better conditions; the corporations would provide what their workers were organizing to demand and in doing so circumvent and undercut the power of organized labor (Mosher 1995:90–91).

A form of paternalism existed in some late-nineteenth- and early-twentieth-century industries in the United States. The factory and the commu-

Figure C.1. Children playing in the back yard of workers' housing in Woonsocket, Rhode Island. For Child Welfare Exhibit, 1912–13. Library of Congress, GIG-NCLC-02707.

nity were portrayed as a family with shared interests; however, the owner always determined what was in the best interest of the community and the factory, and the threat of force always stood in the balance. "Paternalism," notes Collins (2002:157), "operated through provision of non-wage goods and services, an ideology of beneficence, and the cultivation of deferential relations between company and its employees. . . . Through such means, paternalism had the effect of transforming power relations into moral obligations—a system of mutual responsibilities, duties, and, ultimately, even rights." One strategy used by industrialists was creating a family work force. This pressured all family members to work efficiently, knowing that if they did not, the jobs held by other family members could be jeopardized (Collins 2002). A sense of paternalism also meant that workers overlooked some work-related hazards. In return, they believed that they were entitled to job security and improved wages and working conditions (Collins 2002:158).

Many historians see paternalism as a way of caring for families and communities by providing employment. Others see paternalism as a way of creating "white slaves" who had few liberties and a low wage. Jane Collins (2002:166–167) points out that there is an increasing number of anthropologists who are focusing on issues such as creolization and diaspora studies.

She suggests that perhaps a similar approach can be performed on workers' concerns and needs with the current development of transnational industries.

Clearly, working-class people see their rights and power eroding. A 2005 survey sponsored by the AFL-CIO (American Federation of Labor and Congress of Industrial Organizations) of workers nationwide is telling. While newspaper headlines boasted of a recovering economy, the majority of American workers (54 percent) were concerned about their economic situation (in 1999, 70 percent of those surveyed were hopeful or confident). While the American dream is that each generation does better than the last, a majority of workers (53 percent) in the survey felt that they were not as well off or were about the same as their parents. They felt that their income was not keeping up with the cost of living, with health care and rising energy costs as the major factors. Only three in ten workers were satisfied with the health-care system, and seven in ten wanted to see the federal government guarantee health-care coverage (Hart Research Associates 2005).

With the globalization of industrial work, many of the historical issues discussed above continue in communities around the world, such as the millions of bonded child laborers from the Indian Dalits, the so-called untouchables. In the 1980s and 1990s the World Bank heavily financed silk reeling and twisting in India without monitoring or placing restrictions on the use of bonded child labor, even though the silk industry relies heavily on it (Human Rights Watch 2003:6, 21, 46). Some scholars see contemporary child labor influenced by cultural traditions. For instance, Madiha Murshed (2001) sees child labor in Pakistan today as a common cultural practice among the lower castes; as in the nineteenth century in the United States, Pakistani people see child labor as a rite of passage into adulthood. It is a social norm with little or no social stigma to the family (Basu 1999). As with the Italian immigrants interviewed in Boston Harbor in 1919, these cultural activities are so ingrained that alternative behaviors are not seen as appropriate.

According to the U.S. Department of the State there are fifty thousand people trafficked into the United States every year for the purpose of working in sweatshops, brothels, fields, and even private homes (Powell 2002). These stories are often underplayed in the press and in public history displays. However, in April 1998, the Smithsonian Institution took a bold step to address this issue and opened a temporary exhibit titled "Between a Rock and a Hard Place: A History of American Sweatshops, 1820–present." The exhibit discussed how young women from Thai villages are deceived into coming to the United States to work in sweatshops by ringleaders in their native land. The exhibit faced opposition from clothing manufacturers who tried to block its opening. The manufacturers' reaction led museums in San Francisco, Chicago, and New York to cancel the exhibit when it was scheduled to travel later that year (Saunders 1999).

Teaching with Historic Places

The story of labors' struggle and the impact on working-class families often is omitted from the national consciousness and from school curriculums (Cobble and Kessler-Harris 1993). With the weakening of the labor movement, many fear that people will forget the hard-fought battles for justice in pay and working and living conditions. Historian Howard Zinn (2003:54), for instance, questions why the story of the Colorado Coalfield War, which cast a dark shadow on American corporate capitalism, is not included in history textbooks while the books celebrate John D. Rockefeller's building of Standard Oil. Americans choose to remember the building of corporations rather than the impact and events associated with their failings. To emphasize class struggle is considered bold and even radical, but in fact class struggle is very much part of America today. These difficult histories are important stories that need to be installed at national public places in order to make people more aware of the many inequities that still exist.

There are ways to make the teaching of labor history and labor archaeology accessible to teachers and students. The Teaching with Historic Places program administered by the National Park Service offers lesson plans for teachers and exercises for students. Developed by professionals familiar with the particular resource, the teaching plans allow students and teachers to explore important issues in our past that are linked to significant places on the American landscape. These lesson plans are developed for sites that are listed on the National Register of Historic Places, and some of these are places where we can learn more about labor's heritage in Americans. The lessons are available on the Internet and are ready for immediate classroom use (www.nps.gov/history/nr/twhp/descrip.htm). A sample of lesson plans related to labor history and labor archaeology follows.

The "Johnson Lake Mine: Mining for Tungsten in Nevada's Snake Range" lesson explores the mining and uses of tungsten at the turn of the twentieth century and shows how archaeology can be used to learn more about this

Figure C.2. Restored clock tower at the Boott Mills, Lowell, Massachusetts, 1998.
Photograph by Paul A. Shackel.

industrial site and its associated community. The lesson plan outlines the basic processes for mining tungsten and the significance of mining tungsten during the World War I era.

"Saugus Iron Works: Life and Work at an Early American Industrial Site" encourages students to investigate the remains of colonial America's first fully integrated iron works and examine seventeenth-century daily life in the iron works. Archaeology is used to explore the past, and the lesson describes the development of America's early iron industry. It discusses the important considerations made when determining the location and development of the iron works. In a similar fashion, "Hopewell Furnace: A Pennsylvania Iron-making Plantation Lesson Plan" explores Hopewell's development and the importance of the surrounding natural resources. It describes the steps in making iron and iron products and shows how the type of work one performed helped determine social status within the Hopewell community.

"Building America's Industrial Revolution: The Boott Cotton Mills of Lowell, MA" describes how water-powered technology applied to textile mills in early nineteenth-century New England revolutionized industry. This new technology changed mill architecture, city planning, and transportation (Figure C.2). Mechanics Hall, located in Worcester, Massachusetts, in the Blackstone River Valley National Heritage Corridor, is the focus of another lesson plan from the industrial Northeast. "Mechanics Hall: Symbols of Pride and Industry" provides an overview of how the industrial revolution changed New England's communities along this once quiet river valley.

Patterson, New Jersey, was initially developed in 1792, with the support of Alexander Hamilton and other investors, as a planned industrial community. By the middle of the following century it became known as Silk City because of its tremendous output of silk weavings. "Patterson, New Jersey: America's Silk City" provides an overview of the silk industry and describes the impact of the 1913 silk industry strike. The lesson plan explains the lives of the mill owners and the workers and provides an overview of workers' discontent when increased automation meant fewer jobs and more work for machine tenders. The strike was eventually broken, serving as a devastating blow to the Industrial Workers of the World. The strike is also remembered as part of workers' struggle for anti–child labor legislation, safety in the workplace, a minimum wage, and reasonable working hours.

Making the Study of Industry Public

While there are several lesson plans that can be used to teach about labor's heritage, there are many places on the American landscape where we can learn about our industrial past. Visiting these places can help us understand life and work in an industrial capitalist system. However, it is always important to critically view how work, labor, and industry are being interpreted in public places. What follows is a small sample of places that may be worth visiting.

Mining

In the American Southwest, many of the company mining towns and large labor encampments from the late nineteenth century followed a grid pattern that reflected order and rationality, while the smaller towns formed in linear strips along roadways. Some of these places still survive, either as inhabited towns or abandoned places visible from the roadside. Tens of thousands of abandoned mines are scattered throughout the region. In Colorado alone there are twenty-three thousand inactive and abandoned mines and mining communities. The mines are mostly unsafe and contain unstable soil, unsafe roofs and ladders, deadly gasses, poisonous snakes, and dangerous explosives. However, throughout the region there are a handful of places that are stabilized and safe and encourage heritage tourism.

Tyrone, New Mexico, is one place that thrived for a short time, financed largely by the Phelps Dodge Corporation. Bertram Goodhue, a well-known architect who designed the buildings of the Panama-Pacific Exposition in San Diego in 1915, helped design the town, which included business and residential areas, a school, and a hospital. Tyrone has several mansions that are influenced by the Mediterranean rococo style. Following a sharp drop in copper prices not long after the town was completed in 1915, the town was abandoned. Showing some age from a lack of upkeep, many of the building still stand, and a newer part of town is located nearby.

Cokedale, located in southern Colorado, is coal camp that has many surviving domestic structures as well as the remains of coke ovens. Founded in 1906 by the American Smelting and Refining Company, at its peak it contained fifteen hundred residents. The town thrived until the end of World War II, when the demand for coal and coke dwindled. Operations ceased in 1946, and miners and families could then buy their homes. Cokedale was placed on the National Historic Register in 1984. Today, about 125 people reside in the town and are making an effort to create an industrial tourist attraction. Cokedale has a museum that illustrates the coalfield troubles of 1913–14, although the town's reconstruction romanticizes Colorado's coal mining history (www.sangres.com/colorado/lasanimas/cokedale.htm).

Mining also occurred in other regions of the United States, and Buxton, Iowa, is a compelling story of a predominantly African American mining town. African Americans were generally disenfranchised from industrial labor after Emancipation, but when Caucasian workers at Mucakinock, Iowa, struck for higher wages, the Consolidation Coal Company recruited African Americans from Virginia. By 1881 there were more than four thousand African Americans working in the mining town. The operation was later abandoned and relocated to Buxton, along with the work force and supporting community. Buxton flourished for several decades but was abandoned in 1923 when the mining operations ceased (www.blackiowa.org/exhibits/exhibits/buxton.html).

Copper and iron mine communities once forged a mighty industry in the Great Lakes region. Many of these places are closed, but a few have been stabilized and are interpreted for the public. Keweenaw National Historical Park, located in the Upper Peninsular of Michigan, celebrates and interprets the copper mining industry (www.nps.gov/kewe). The park preserves the heritage of copper mining in a setting where many of the original structures and landscapes of the copper era are still present. The interpretation shows how copper mining built thriving industries in a remote region of the United States. Copper mines in the Upper Peninsular lured immigrants from distant places, employing people from more than thirty different ethnic groups. The architecture and design of the factories is an example of a corporate-sponsored community that was common in early American industry. The archaeology sites in the region contain the oldest known mines in the Western Hemisphere, dating back some seven thousand years. However, historic copper mining in this region pioneered technological advancements that were used for mining throughout the world. Other places, such as Klondike Gold Rush National Historical Park, are closely associated with the mining industry in Alaska (www.nps.gov/klgo). Several archaeology reports exist on the archaeology of domestic structures in the park.

Saltpeter is a mineral that is extracted when sediments are leached with water. Beginning in the 1770s, caves in the upper South were mined for their saltpeter as a response to the need for gunpowder during the American Revolution. Mining increased significantly during the War of 1812, but production slowed after 1815. When the price of saltpeter dropped significantly with the emergence of world markets, mines were quickly abandoned. Because of the quick abandonment and the dry and cool climate conditions in these caves, many of the industrial complexes associated with saltpeter extraction are well preserved (Douglas 2001:252–253; Duncan 1997:91). Mammoth Cave in Kentucky is one of these places. There, saltpeter extraction peaked during the War of 1812, but the cave still holds the remains of this industry. About seventy enslaved African American worked in Mammoth Cave collecting soil and bringing it to leaching vats in the cave. Wooden pipes carried water to flood the vats, and after the water had absorbed the calcium nitrate from the soil, it was pumped to the surface, leached through wood ash, and then boiled until saltpeter crystals formed. The slaves then packed the saltpeter in barrels and shipped it to gunpowder manufacturers (www.nps.gov/maca). A historic tour of Mammoth Cave will take you by some of the manufacturing ruins of the saltpeter industry.

In the East, the Eckley Miners' Village, near Hazleton, Pennsylvania, interprets the everyday lives of anthracite miners and their families. It is one of many mining towns, or "patches," built in the anthracite region of Pennsylvania. Mining began in 1854 at Eckley, and beginning in 1890 strip mining took place around the town. In 1969, the Huss Coal Company sold Eckley to a group of businessmen who then deeded the land over to the state in 1971. Today, fewer than two dozen people reside in Eckley. The associated museum illustrates the hardships of life in a mining community, such as impoverishment, illness, accidents, death, and labor discontent. Visitors can see museum exhibits and walk through the old mining village (www.eckleyminers.org).

Industries and Mills

Blackstone River Valley National Heritage Corridor celebrates the birth of the industrial revolution in the United States. The Blackstone River runs from Worcester, Massachusetts, to Providence, Rhode Island, and it includes Slater Mill, the first successful cotton-spinning factory in the United States (www.nps.gov/blac). Slater's success encouraged others to develop water-powered textile mills on the Blackstone River, and eventually others followed along various rivers in New England. Capitalists built mills, homes, schools, and churches for their workers.

Planned cities developed that originally recruited mill girls to tend to the machinery, and by the late nineteenth century many of the larger New England towns were receiving immigrants from Southern and Eastern Europe. Today, the city of Lowell, Massachusetts, embraces its industrial past. Lowell National Historical Park provides an overview of the rise and fall of the

New England industry (www.nps.gov/lowe). One exhibit extols the material benefits of industry, but the exhibit also explains labor strife. In addition, visitors are invited to walk through the mill with earplugs while more than one hundred machines operate simultaneously. The experience is enough to make one realize the strain on the mill girls (and later immigrants) as they labored ten hours per day.

Woonsocket, Rhode Island, attracted Canadians from the Quebec region, and in the nineteenth century it became a predominantly French-speaking city. Its story is told in the Museum of Work and Culture in Woonsocket (www.nps.gov/blac/planyourvisit/visitor-centers-mowc.htm). As you move through the exhibits you can read about and listen to the workers' stories and learn about how they coped with substandard work and living conditions. This museum exhibition effectively discusses the historical development of labor and class and shows the impact of industrialization on work, domestic life-styles, and health conditions.

Clashes between labor and capital occurred throughout the nineteenth and twentieth centuries, and the Lawrence Heritage State Park contains a restored 1840s boardinghouse and interprets one of the most powerful labor struggles in the twentieth century, the 1912 Bread and Roses Strike, which took place in Lawrence (www.mass.gov/dcr/parks/northeast/lwhp.htm). Immigrant women from thirty different nationalities struck in Lawrence for better wages and improved work conditions. In sympathy, the strike spread throughout the Northeast, closing many of the textile industries (Figure C.3). Those industries eventually left the Northeast, and Lawrence is now one of the poorest cities in Massachusetts, suffering from the loss of its major economic base. Today, there are mixed reactions to remembering this strike, although an annual Bread and Roses festival remembers the event and strives to interest nontraditional communities in labor's heritage. The festival, which takes place on Labor Day, promotes the city as having a "special place in American labor history, and as the quintessential 'Immigrant City,' both past and present."

Several exhibitions at Harpers Ferry National Historical Park interpret nineteenth-century industry in the town. One exhibition focuses on the early industrial development of Harpers Ferry, describing some of the machinery found in the early armory. This exhibition is occasionally staffed, and interpreters demonstrate how to operate the armory's historic wood lathe. Across the room is a display that shows the different types of water power used in nineteenth-century Harpers Ferry. Another exhibit in Lower Town illustrates how armory workers may have practiced their craft in a

Figure C.3. The Bread and Roses Strike with children on the sidewalk in Lawrence, Massachusetts, 1912. George Gratham Bain Collection, Library of Congress, USZ62-98168.

piecework system at home until about 1841, when the military took control of the facility and made all workers abide by a standard work discipline. Another exhibit interprets daily life in a working-class boardinghouse. The families that inhabited this and other boardinghouses had a high rate of disease, indicated by the high concentration of parasites found in the privy, and they relied heavily on self-medication. A walking trail through an archaeological preserve known as Virginius Island provides an overview of a nineteenth-century mill village. (www.nps.gov/hafe/index.htm)

Founded by Col. James Withers Sloss, the Sloss Furnaces in Birmingham, Alabama, opened in 1882 and operated under various other names until it closed in 1971. It was a pig iron–producing blast furnace, and by the early twentieth century it had become one of the largest sellers of pig iron in the world. The majority of its workers were African Americans, although working conditions were segregated and whites held the managerial and skilled positions. At the turn of the twentieth century the company built forty-eight cottages to house African American workers and their families, a community that became known as Sloss Quarters. The introduction of convict labor in 1928 hurt the low-paid wage labor, which for the most part was being performed by African Americans. In 1971 the land and furnace were donated to the state of Alabama and the Sloss Furnace Association lobbied to save it form demolition on the grounds that it was a symbol of the technology that made Birmingham the industrial center of the South.

Now owned by the city, it is a National Historic Landmark and is preserved for public use with an interpretive museum and a metal arts program. The site will become part of a linear park running east-west through downtown Birmingham (www.slossfurnace.com).

Rosie the Riveter/World War II Home Front National Historical Park (www.rosietheriveter.org/) celebrates the sacrifices of the men and women working on the American home front. Women who worked in the defense industries became known as "Rosie the Riveters" after a popular song written in 1942. The national park is located in the wartime boomtown of Richmond, California, which has the nation's largest concentration of intact World War II historic structures. Together these structures can illustrate a broad spectrum of wartime home-front stories. The park is also committed to collecting a wide range of stories that relate to the American home front. It includes a Rosie the Riveter memorial and a host of other industrial buildings around the harbor.

Throughout the United States there are many places that celebrate the development of railroads, and scenic tours are provided on older steam locomotives through the countryside. The Steamtown National Historic site provides an overview of steam-powered locomotives in the American experience (www.nps.gov/stea). Other places, such as the Nevada Northern Railway Museum in Ely, Nevada (www.nevadanorthernrailway.net), interpret the development of the railroad as it served the newly developed copper mining industry in the region in the 1890s. Ely was the southern terminus of a short line that connected to the rails of the Central Pacific. Tracks ran another ten miles west to the mines. Today, catering to tourism, there are three train rides daily. The Nevada Northern Railway East Ely yard complex, locomotives and rolling stock in Ely, is listed as a National Historic Landmark because it is "the best-preserved, least altered, and most complete main yard complex remaining from the steam railroad era." For fans of steam engine rides and beautiful scenery, check out the excursions from Chama, New Mexico (Cumbres and Toltec Scenic Railroad; www.cumbres toltec.com), and Durango, Colorado (Durango and Silverton Narrow Gauge Railroad; www.durangosilvertonrailroad.com), which wind through beautiful scenery overlooking valleys and squeezing between mountains.

Some Thoughts

Since the urban and agricultural revolutions, no other societal development has changed the way people use the earth's resources or changed the way humans work and live more than the industrial revolution. Reminders of this transformation are visible on the landscape across America as abandoned mills, factories, and mines. These landscapes also serve as a reminder of the nation's former industrial prowess. While these landscapes beg for interpretation, a part of this history is no longer accessible, as many of the workers, their families, and their descendants have moved elsewhere. The history is inaccessible, poorly documented, or even paved over.

Industry is an important part of our national story, and this book has provided a brief sketch of several studies that allow for labor's heritage to have a place in the national public memory. But for the most part histories are selected and particular viewpoints are emphasized to create a past that is both factual and yet partial. Michael Kammen (1991:3) reminds us that "societies in fact reconstruct their pasts rather than faithfully record them, and that they do so with the needs of contemporary culture clearly in mind—manipulating the past in order to mold the present." Deindustrialization in the United States and the mobilization of capital has meant the dissolution of communities and the weakening of union labor. With industrial signatures remaining on the landscape, it is important to recognize that labor's heritage has a place in our national story. It has been part of the American experience, and further research will help us understand labor's past and how it is remembered today. How industrial places are interpreted to the public will be a struggle for generations to come as tensions between labor and capital remain, and the fight to control the interpretation of these places will continue.

References Cited

Aitken, Hugh G. J.

1985   *Scientific Management in Action: Taylorism at Watertown Arsenal, 1908–1915.* Princeton, N.J.: Princeton University Press.

Alexander, John K.

1980   *Render Them Submissive: Responses to Poverty in Philadelphia, 1760–1800.* Amherst: University of Massachusetts Press.

Bassett, Everett

1994   Gender, Social Organization, and Wage Labor among the Apache. In *Those of Little Note*, edited by Elizabeth M. Scott, 55–79. Tucson: University of Arizona Press.

Basu, Kaushik

1999   Child Labor: Cause, Consequence, and Culture, with Remarks on International Labor Standards. *Journal of Economic Literature* 37:1083–1119.

Baxter, Jane Eva

2007   *Landscapes through the Looking Glass: Pullman's Industrial Landscape as the Presentation of a Social Ideal.* Williamsburg, Va.: Society for Historical Archaeology.

Baxter, R. Scott

2002   Industrial and Domestic Landscapes of a California Oil Field. *Historical Archaeology* 36 (3): 18–27.

Baxter, R. Scott, and Rebecca Allen

2002   Archaeological Investigations of Life within the Woolen Mills Chinatown, San Jose. In *The Chinese in America: A History from Gold Mountain to the New Millennium*, edited by Susie Lan Cassel, 381–398. Walnut Creek, Calif.: AltaMira Press.

Beaudry, Mary C.

1989   The Lowell Boott Mills Complex and Its Housing: Material Expressions of Corporate Ideology. *Historical Archaeology* 23 (1): 19–32.

1987   The Boott Cotton Mills Corporation Mill Yard and Housing: Material Expressions of Industrial Capitalism. In *Interdisciplinary Investigations of the Boott Mills, Lowell, Massachusetts.* Vol. 2, *The Kirk Street Agent's House*, edited by Mary C. Beaudry and Stephen A. Mrozowski, 9–14. Cultural Resources Management Study 19. United States Department of the Interior, National Park Service, North Atlantic Regional Office, Boston.

Beaudry, Mary C., Lauren J. Cook, and Stephen A. Mrozowski

1991   Artifacts as Active Voices: Material Culture as Social Discourse. In *The Archaeology of Inequality*, edited by Randall H. McGuire and Robert Paynter, 150–191. New York: Basil Blackwell.

Beaudry, Mary C., and Stephen A. Mrozowski

1989   The Archaeology of Work and Home Life in Lowell, Massachusetts: An Interdisciplinary Study of the Boott Cotton Mills Corporation. *IA: The Journal of the Society for Industrial Archaeology* 19 (2): 1–22.

Beecher, Catherine E., and Harriet Beecher Stowe

1994   [1869] *The American Woman's Home; or, Principles of Domestic Science; Being A Guide to the Formation and Maintenance of Economical, Healthful, Beautiful and Christian Homes*. Originally published in 1869. Hartford, Conn.: Stowe-Day Foundation.

Blewett, Mary

1979   The National Park Service Meets the Working People of Lowell. *Labor and Community Newsletter* 1:2–3.

Blight, David

2001   *Race and Reunion: The Civil War in American Memory*. Cambridge: Harvard University Press.

Bond, Kathleen H.

1989   The Medicine, Alcohol, and Soda Vessels from the Boott Mills. In *Interdisciplinary Investigations of the Boott Mills, Lowell, Massachusetts, Vol.3: The Boarding House System as a Way of Life*, edited by Mary C. Beaudry and Stephen A. Mrozowski, 121–140. Cultural Resources Management Study 21. United States Department of the Interior, National Park Service, North Atlantic Regional Office, Boston.

Boomhower, Ray E.

2002   New Harmony: Home to Indiana's Communal Societies. *Traces of Indiana and Midwestern History* 14 (4): 36–37.

Bourdieu, Pierre

1977   *Outline of a Theory of Practice*. New York: Cambridge University Press.

Boydston, Jeanne

1990   *Home and Work: Housework, Wages, and the Ideology of Labor in the Early Republic*. New York: Oxford University Press.

Brandon, Jamie C., and James M. Davidson

2005   The Landscape of Van Winkle's Mill: Identity, Myth, and Modernity in the Ozark Upland South. *Historical Archaeology* 39 (3): 113–131.

Brashler, Janet G.

1991   When Daddy Was a Shanty Boy: The Role of Gender in the Organization of the Logging Industry in Highland West Virginia. In *Gender in Historical Archaeology*, edited by Donna J. Seifert. *Historical Archaeology* 25 (4): 54–68.

Braudel, Fernand

1979a   *The Structures of Everyday Life: Civilization and Capitalism, 15th–18th Century*. Vol. 1. New York: Harper and Row.

1979b *The Wheels of Commerce: Civilization and Capitalism, 15th–18th Century.* Vol. 2. New York: Harper and Row.

1979c *Perspectives of the World: Civilization and Capitalism, 15th–18th Century.* Vol. 3. New York: Harper and Row.

Brody, David

1993 *In Labor's Cause: Main Themes on the History of the American Worker.* New York: Oxford University Press.

1989 Labor History, Industrial Relations, and the Crisis of American Labor. *Industrial and Labor Relations Review* 43 (1): 5–18.

1980 Labor History in the 1980s: Toward a History of the American Worker. In *The Past Before Us: Contemporary Historical Writing in the United States*, edited by Michael Kammen, 252–269. Ithaca, N.Y.: Cornell University Press.

1979 The Old Labor History and the New. *Labor History* 20 (1): 111–121.

Brown, Richard D.

1989 *Knowledge Is Power: The Diffusion of Information in Early America, 1700–1865.* New York: Oxford University Press.

Bruno, Robert

1998 Working, Playing, and Fighting for Control: Steelworkers and Shopfloor Identity. *Labor Studies Journal* 2 (1): 3–30.

Burley, David V.

1989 Function, Meaning and Context: Ambiguities in Ceramic Use by the Hivernant Metis of the Northwest Plains. *Historical Archaeology* 23 (1): 97–106.

Bushman, Richard L.

1992 *The Refinement of America: Persons, Houses, Cities.* New York: Knopf.

Butler, William B.

1999 The Grand Lake Lodge Sawmill, Rocky Mountain National Park, Grand County, Colorado. *Southwest Lore* 65 (1): 19–42.

Campbell, Collin

1987 *The Romantic Ethic and the Spirit of Modern Consumerism.* New York: Basil Blackwell.

Candee, Richard M.

1992 Early New England Mill Towns of the Piscataqua River Valley. In *The Company Town: Architecture and Society in the Early Industrial Age*, edited by John S. Garner, 111–138. New York: Oxford University Press.

Caplinger, Michael

1997 *Bridges Over Time: A Technological Context for the Baltimore and Ohio Railroad Main Stem at Harpers Ferry, West Virginia.* Morgantown, W.Va.: Institute for the History of Technology and Industrial Archaeology.

Carlson, Stephen P.

1991 *First Iron Works: A History of the First Iron Works Association.* Saugus, Mass.: Saugus Historical Society.

Carlton, David L.

1982 *Mill and Town in South Carolina, 1880–1920.* Baton Rouge: Louisiana State University Press.

Casella, Eleanor
2007   *The Archaeology of Institutional Confinement.* Gainesville: University Press of Florida.
2001   To Watch or Restrain: Female Convict Prisons in 19th Century Tasmania. *International Journal of Historical Archaeology* 5 (1): 45–72.

Casella, Eleanor C., and James Symonds, eds.
2005   *Industrial Archaeology: Future Directions.* New York: Springer.

Cassell, Mark S., ed.
2005   Landscapes of Industrial Labor. *Historical Archaeology* 39 (3).

Cate, Eliza J.
1848   The Factories of Lowell and the Factory Girls. *New England Offering* 2:26–28

Chan, Sucheng, ed.
1991   *Entry Denied: Exclusion and the Chinese Community in America, 1882–1943.* Philadelphia: Temple University Press.

Chernow, Ron
1998   *Titan: The Life of John D. Rockefeller, Sr.* New York: Random House.

Childs, S. Terry
1998   "Find the Ekijunjumira": Iron Mine Discovery, Ownership and Power among the Toro of Uganda. In *Social Approaches to an Industrial Past,* edited by A. Bernard Knapp, Vincent C. Pigott, and Eugenia W. Herbert, 123–137. New York: Routledge.

Choy, Philip P
1995   *The Coming Man: 19th Century American Perceptions of the Chinese.* Seattle: University of Washington Press.

Christian, Marcus B.
1972   *Negro Ironworkers in Louisiana, 1718–1900.* Gretna, La.: Pelican.

Clark, Christopher
1996   Rural America and the Transition to Capitalism. *Journal of the Early Republic* 16 (2): 223–236.

Clark, C. M.
1987   Trouble at T'Mill: Industrial Archaeology in the 1980s. *Antiquity* 61 (232): 169–179.

Cobble, Dorothy Sue, and Alice Kessler-Harris
1993   The New Labor History in American History Textbooks. *Journal of American History* 79 (4): 1534–1545.

Collins, Jane
2002   Deterritorialization and Workplace Culture. *American Ethnologist* 29 (1): 151–171.

Costello, Julia G.
1998   Bread Fresh from the Oven: Memories of Italian Breadbaking in the California Mother Lode. In *Archaeologists as Storytellers,* edited by Adrian Praetzellis and Mary Praetzellis. *Historical Archaeology* 32 (1): 66–73.

Costello, Julia G., and Mary L. Maniery
1988 *Rice Bowls in the Delta: Artifacts Recovered from the 1915 Asian Community of Walnut Grove, California*. Occasional Paper 16. UCLA Institute of Archaeology, Los Angeles.

Cotter, John L., Roger W. Moss, Bruce C. Gill, and Jiyul Kim
1988 *The Walnut Street Prison Workshop*. Philadelphia: Anthenaeum of Philadelphia.

Cotter, John L., Daniel Roberts, and Michael Parrington
1992 *The Buried Past: An Archaeological History of Philadelphia*. Philadelphia: University of Pennsylvania Press.

Council, R. Bruce, Nicholas Honerkamp, and M. Elizabeth Will
1992 *Industry and Technology in Antebellum Tennessee: The Archaeology of Bluff Furnace*. Knoxville: University of Tennessee Press.

Cowan, Ruth S.
1983 *More Work for Mother: The Ironies of Household Technology from the Open Hearth to the Microwave*. New York: Basic Books.

Cressey, Pamela, John Stephens, Steven Shephard, and Barbara Magid
1982 The Core Periphery Relationship and the Archaeological Record in Alexandria, Virginia. In *Archaeology of Urban America: The Search for Pattern and Process*, edited by Roy S. Dickens, 143–174. New York: Academic Press.

Cromley, Elizabeth C.
1989 *Alone Together: A History of New York's Early Apartment*. Ithaca, N.Y.: Cornell University Press.

Crowell, Aron L.
1997 *Archaeology and the Capitalist World System: A Study from Russian America*. New York: Plenum Press.

Cummings, Linda Scott
1994 Diet and Prehistoric Landscape During the Nineteenth and Early Twentieth Centuries at Harpers Ferry, West Virginia: A View from the Old Master Armorer's Complex. In *An Archaeology of Harpers Ferry's Commercial and Residential District*, edited by Paul A. Shackel and Susan E. Winter. *Historical Archaeology* 28 (4): 94–105.

Cunningham, Hugh
2000 The Decline of Child Labor: Labor Markets and Family Economics in Europe and North America since 1830. *Economic History Review* 53:409–428.

Dabakis, Melissa
1998 *Monuments of Manliness: Visualizing Labor in American Sculpture, 1880–1935*. New York: Cambridge University Press.

Dalzell, Robert F.
1987 *Enterprising Elite: The Boston Associates and the World They Made*. Cambridge: Harvard University Press.

Davis, Devra Lee
2002a *When Smoke Ran Like Water: Tales of Environmental Deception and the Battle Against Pollution*. New York: Basic Books.

2002b The Heavy Air of Donora, Pa. *Chronicle Review: The Chronicle of Higher Education*, sec. 2, pp. B7–B12.

Deagan, Kathleen

1987 *Artifacts of the Spanish Colonies of Florida and the Caribbean, 1500–1800.* Washington, D.C.: Smithsonian Institution Press.

1985 Spanish-Indian Interaction in Sixteenth-Century Florida and Hispaniola. In *Cultures in Contact: The Impact of European Contacts on Native American Cultural Institutions, A.D. 1000–1800*, edited by W. W. Fitzhugh, 281–318. Washington, D.C.: Smithsonian Institution Press.

1983 *Spanish St. Augustine: The Archaeology of a Colonial Creole Community.* New York: Academic Press.

1978 The Material Assemblage of 16th-Century Spanish Florida. *Historical Archaeology* 12:25–50.

1973 *Mestizaje* in Colonial St. Augustine. *Ethnohistory* 20 (1): 55–65.

Deagan, Kathleen, and Darcie MacMahon

1995 *Fort Mose: Colonial America's Black Fortress of Freedom.* Gainesville: University Press of Florida/Florida Museum of Natural History.

DeCunzo, Lu Ann

1995 Reform, Respite, Ritual: An Archaeology of Institutions; The Magdalen Society of Philadelphia, 1800–1850. *Historical Archaeology* 29 (3): iii–168.

Deetz, James

1996 *In Small Things Forgotten: The Archaeology of Early American Life.* Charlottesville: University Press of Virginia.

1963 Archaeological Investigations at La Purisima Mission. In *UCLA Archaeological Survey Annual Report, 1962–1963*, 163–208. Los Angeles: UCLA Institute of Archaeology.

DeForest, Robert, and Lawrence Veiller

1970 *Tenement House Problem.* Originally published 1903. New York: Arno Press.

Delle, James A.

1998 *An Archaeology of Social Space: Analyzing a Coffee Plantation in Jamaica's Blue Mountains.* New York: Plenum.

Denkler, Ann

2007 *Sustaining Identity, Recapturing Heritage: Exploring Issues of Public History, Tourism, and Race in a Southern Town.* Lanham, Md.: Lexington Books.

2001 Sustaining Identity, Recapturing Heritage: Exploring Issues of Public History, Tourism, and Race in a Southern Rural Town. Ph.D. diss., American Studies, University of Maryland, College Park.

Dew, Charles B.

1994a *Bonds of Iron: Master and Slave at Buffalo Forge.* New York: W. W. Norton.

1994b David Ross and the Oxford Iron Works: A Study of Industrial Slavery in the Early Nineteenth-Century South. *William and Mary Quarterly* 31 (2): 189–224.

1966 *Ironmaking to the Confederacy: Joseph R. Anderson and the Tredegan Iron Works.* New Haven, Conn.: Yale University Press.

Donnelly, Colm J., and Audrey J. Horning
2002   Post-Medieval and Industrial Archaeology in Ireland: An Overview. *Antiquity* 76 (2): 557–561.

Douglas, Joseph C.
2001   Miners and Moonshiners: Historic Industrial Uses of Tennessee Caves. *Midcontinental Journal of Archaeology MCJA* 26 (2): 251–267.

Dublin, Thomas
1979   *Women at Work: The Transformation of Work and Community in Lowell, Massachusetts, 1826–1860.* New York: Columbia University Press.
1977   Women, Work, and Protest in the Early Lowell Mills: "The Oppressing Hand of Avarice Would Enslave Us." In *Class, Sex, and the Women Worker,* edited by Milton Cantor and Bruce Ware, 43–63. Westport, Conn.: Greenwood Press.

Dubofsky, Melvyn
2000   *Hard Work: The Making of Labor History.* Urbana: University of Illinois Press.
1996   *Industrialism and the American Worker: 1865–1920.* Wheeling, Ill.: Harlan Davidson.

Du Bois, W. E. B.
1935   *Black Reconstruction in America.* Cleveland: Harcourt, Brace.

Duncan, M. Susan
1997   Examining Early Nineteenth Century Saltpeter Caves: An Archaeological Perspective. *Journal of Cave and Karst Studies* 59 (2): 91–94.

Eaton, Clement
1961   *The Growth of Southern Civilization, 1790–1860.* New York: Harper and Brothers.

Edensor, Tim
2005   *Industrial Ruins: Spaces, Aesthetics and Materiality.* New York: Berg.

Elliott, John H.
1994   Chinese Mining Camp Archaeological Site, Warren Mining District 01IH1961. National Register Nomination. On file, U.S. Department of the Interior, National Park Service, Washington, D.C.

Ellison, Ralph
1952   *The Invisible Man.* New York: Random House.

Emmons, David M.
1989   *The Butte Irish: Class and Ethnicity in an American Mining Town, 1875–1925.* Urbana: University of Illinois Press.

Faler, Paul G.
1981   *Mechanics and Manufacturers in the Early Industrial Revolution: Lynn, Massachusetts, 1780–1860.* Albany: State University of New York Press.

Ferguson, Leland G.
1992   *Uncommon Ground: Archaeology and Colonial African America.* Washington, D.C.: Smithsonian Institution Press.

Fink, Leon
1991   "Intellectuals" versus "Workers": Academic Requirements and the Creation of Labor History. *American Historical Review* 96 (2): 396–399.

Fitts, Robert K.

2000 The Five Points Reformed, 1865–1900. In *Tales of Five Points: Working-Class Life in Nineteenth-Century New York*. Vol. 1, *A Narrative History and Archaeology of Block 160*, edited by Rebecca Yamin, 67–90. West Chester, Pa.: John Milner Associates.

Fitzhugh, William W., ed.

1985 *Cultures in Contact: The Impact of European Contacts on Native American Cultural Institutions, A.D. 1000–1800*. Washington, D.C.: Smithsonian Institution Press.

Fitzpatrick, Ellen

1991 Rethinking the Intellectual Origins of American Labor History. *American Historical Review* 96 (2): 422–428.

Foner, Philip S., ed.

1977 *The Factory Girls*. Urbana: University of Illinois Press.

Foner, Philip, and Ronald Lewis, eds.

1989 *Black Workers: A Documentary History from Colonial Times to the Present*. Philadelphia: Temple University Press.

Fonse-Wolf, Ken

1996 From Craft to Industrial Unionism in the Window-Glass Industry: Clarksburg, West Virginia, 1900–1937. *Labor History* 37 (1): 28–49.

Foote, Kenneth E.

1997 *Shadowed Ground: America's Landscapes of Violence and Tragedy*. Austin: University of Texas Press.

Ford, Benjamin

1994 The Health and Sanitation of Postbellum Harpers Ferry. In *An Archaeology of Harpers Ferry's Commercial and Residential District*, edited by Paul A. Shackel and Susan E. Winter. *Historical Archaeology* 28 (4): 49–61.

Foucault, Michel

1986 Of Other Space. *Diacritics* 16:22–23.

1980 Truth and Power. In *Power/ Knowledge*, edited by Colin Gordon, xx. Hassock, UK: Harvester.

1979 *Discipline and Punish: The Birth of the Prison*. New York: Vintage Books.

1977 *Discipline and Punish: The Birth of the Prison*. Translated by Alan Sheridan 1st American ed. New York: Vintage Books.

Francaviglia, Richard

1992 *Hard Places: Reading the Landscapes of America's Historic Mining Districts*. Baltimore: Johns Hopkins University Press.

Garman, James C.

2005 *Detention Castles of Stone and Steel: Landscape, Labor, and the Urban Penitentiary*. Knoxville: University of Tennessee Press.

Gilje, Paul A.

1996 The Rise of Capitalism in the Early Republic. *Journal of the Early Republic* 16 (2): 159–181.

Glassie, Henry

1977   Archaeology and Folklore: Common Anxieties, Common Hopes. In *Historical Archaeology and the Importance of Material Things*, edited by Leland Ferguson, 23–35. Special Publication Series No. 2. Pleasant Hill, Calif.: Society for Historical Archaeology.

Go, Julian, III

1996   Inventing Industrial Accidents and Their Insurance: Discourse and Workers' Compensation in the United States 1880s–1910s. *Social Science History* 20 (3): 401–438.

Gordon, Robert B.

2001   *A Landscape Transformed: The Iron Making District of Salisbury, Connecticut.* New York: Oxford University Press.

Gordon, Robert B., and Patrick M. Malone

1994   *The Texture of Industry: An Archaeological View of Industry in North America.* New York: Oxford University Press.

Gradwohl, David Mayer

2001   Investigations at the Buxton Townsite: A Coal-Mining Community with a Majority Population of African-Americans. *Journal of the Iowa Archaeological Society* 48:95–111.

Gradwohl, David M., and Nancy M. Osborn

1984   *Exploring Buried Buxton: Archaeology of an Abandoned Iowa Coal Mining Town with a Large Black Population.* Ames: Iowa State University Press.

Gratton, Brian, and Jon Moen

2004   Immigration, Culture, and Child Labor in the United States, 1880–1920. *Journal of Interdisciplinary History* 34 (3): 355–391.

Green, James

2000   *Taking History to Heart: The Power of the Past in Building Social Movements.* Amherst: University of Massachusetts Press.

Gunn, T. Butler

1857   The Physiology of New York Boarding-Houses. *Harpers Weekly*, October 10, 652. New York.

Gust, Sherri M.

1993   Animal Bones from Historic Chinese Sites: A Comparison of Sacramento, Woodland, Tucson, Ventura, and Lovelock. In *Hidden Heritage: Historical Archaeology of the Overseas Chinese*, edited by Priscilla Wegars, 177–212. Amityville, N.Y.: Baywood.

Gutman, Herbert

1976   *Work, Culture, and Society in Industrializing America: Essays in American Working Class and Social History.* New York: Knopf.

Gwyn, David

2005   Publishing and Priority in Industrial Archaeology. In *Industrial Archaeology: Future Directions*, edited by Eleanor C. Casella and James Symonds, 121–134. New York: Springer.

Hammond, Bray
1957 *Banks and Politics in America, From the Revolution to the Civil War*. Princeton, N.J.: Princeton University Press.

Hanlan, James P.
1981 *The Working Population of Manchester, New Hampshire 1840–1886*. Ann Arbor, Mich.: UMI Research Press.

Hardesty, Donald
2002 Interpreting Variability and Change in Western Work Camps. *Historical Archaeology* 36 (3): 94–98.

1998 Power and the Industrial Mining Community in the American West. In *Social Approaches to and Industrial Past: The Archaeology and Anthropology of Mining*, edited by A. Bernard Knapp, Vincent C. Pigott, and Eugenia W. Herbert, 81–96. London: Routledge.

1988 *The Archaeology of Mining and Miners: A View from the Silver State*. Society for Historical Archaeology, Special Publication Series, Number 6. California, Pa.

Hareven, Tamara
1982 *Family Time and Industrial Time*. Cambridge: Cambridge University Press.

1978 *Amoskeag: Life and Work in an American Factory City*. New York: Pantheon Books.

Harrington, J. C.
1984 *Archaeology and Enigma of Fort Raleigh*. Raleigh, N.C.: America's Four Hundredth Anniversary Committee.

1966 *An Outwork at Fort Raleigh: Further Archaeological Excavations at Fort Raleigh National Historical Site, North Carolina*. Philadelphia: Eastern Parks and Monuments Association.

1962 *Search for the Cittie of Ralegh: Archaeological Excavations at Fort Raleigh National Historical Site, North Carolina*. Archaeological Research Series no. 6. Washington, D.C.: National Park Service, Department of the Interior.

Harshberger, Patrick
2002 Brooklyn: Review of the 31st Annual Conference. *Society for Industrial Archaeology Newsletter* 31 (3–4): 1–2, 4–5, 7–10.

Hart Research Associates
2005 Labor Day 2005: The State of Working America. Electronic document, http://www.aflcio.org/aboutus/laborday/upload/ld2005_report.pdf (accessed September 10, 2005).

Hartog, Hendrik
1983 *Public Property and Private Power: The Corporation of the City of New York in American Law, 1730–1870*. Chapel Hill: University of North Carolina Press.

Heite, Edward F.
1993 Can Sizes and Waste at the Lebanon Cannery Site: Unscrewing the Inscrutable. *Bulletin, Archaeological Society of Delaware* 30:43–48.

Henderson, Charles R.
1897 *The Social Spirit in America*. New York: Chautauqua Century Press.

Hindle, Brooke, and Steven Lubar

1988　*Engines of Change: The American Industrial Revolution, 1790–1860.* Washington, D.C.: Smithsonian Institution Press.

Hiscox, Michael

2002　Interindustry Factor Mobility and Technological Change: Evidence on Wage and Profit Dispersion across U.S. Industries, 1820–1990. *Journal of Economic History* 62 (2): 383–416.

Holt, Sharon Ann

2006　History Keeps Bethlehem Steel from Going off the Rails: Moving a Complex Community Process toward Success. *Public Historian* 28 (2): 31–44.

Horton, James

2000　Freedom Fighters: African Americans, Slavery, and the Coming Age of the Civil War. Paper presented at the National Park Service Symposium on Strengthening Interpretation of the Civil War Era. Ford's Theater National Historic Site, Washington, D.C.

Howe, Denis E.

1994　Industrial Archaeology: A Survey of Research in New Hampshire. *New Hampshire Archeologist* 33–34 (1): 105–113.

Hudson, Kenneth

1979　*World Industrial Archaeology.* New York: Cambridge University Press.

1978　*Food Clothes and Shelter: Twentieth Century Industrial Archaeology.* London: J. Baker.

1971　*A Guide to the Industrial Archeology of Europe.* Madison, N.J.: Fairleigh Dickinson University Press.

Huey, Paul

1991　The Dutch at Fort Orange. In *Historical Archaeology in Global Perspective*, edited by Lisa Falk, 21–67. Washington, D.C.: Smithsonian Institution Press.

Hull-Walski, Deborah A., and Frank Walski

1994　There's Trouble a-Brewin: The Brewing and Bottling Industries at Harpers Ferry, West Virginia. In *An Archaeology of Harpers Ferry's Commercial and Residential District*, edited by Paul A. Shackel and Susan E. Winter. *Historical Archaeology* 28 (4): 106–121.

Human Rights Watch

2003　India: Small Change; Bonded Child Labor in India's Silk Industry. *Human Rights Watch* 15, no. 2 (January): xx. Electronic document, http://www.hrw.org/reports/2003/india/ (accessed August 6, 2006).

Innes, Stephen

1995　*Creating the Commonwealth: The Economic Culture of Puritan New England.* New York: W. W. Norton.

Jackson, Kenneth T.

1984　The Capital of Capitalism: The New York Metropolitan Region, 1890–1940. In *Metropolis: 1890–1940*, edited by Anthony Sutcliffe, 319–354. Chicago: University of Chicago Press.

Janowitz, Anne
1990   *England's Ruins: Poetic Purpose and the National Landscape*. Cambridge, Mass: Blackwell.
Johnson, Matthew
1996   *An Archaeology of Capitalism*. Cambridge, Mass.: Blackwell.
Jones, Thomas P.
1989 [1827]   The progress of Manufacturers and Internal Improvements in the United States, and Particularly on the Advantages in the manufacturing of Cotton and Other Goods. In *Black Workers: A Documentary History from Colonial Times to the Present*, edited by Philip S. Foner and Ronald L. Lewis, 77–82. Philadelphia: Temple University Press.
Juravich, J.
1985   *Chaos on the Shop Floor*. Philadelphia: Temple University Press.
Kamau, Lucy Jayne
1992   The Anthropology of Space in Harmonist and Owenite New Harmony. *Communal Societies* 12:68–89.
Kammen, Michael
1991   *Mystic Chords of Memory: The Transformation of Tradition in American Culture*. New York: Knopf.
Kelland, Lara
2005   Putting Haymarket to Rest? *Labor: Studies in Working-Class History of the Americas* 2 (2): 21–38.
Kemp, Emery L., ed.
1996   *Industrial Archaeology: Techniques*. Malabar, Fla.: Krieger.
Kemper, Jackson III
n.d.   *American Charcoal Making*. Hopewell Village, Pa.: Eastern National Park and Monument Association.
Kittredge, Mabel Hyde
1911   *Housekeeping Notes: How to Furnish and Keep House in a Tenement Flat*. Boston: Whitcomb and Barrows.
Knapp, A. Bernard
1998   Introduction. In *Social Approaches to and Industrial Past: The Archaeology and Anthropology of Mining*, edited by A. Bernard Knapp, Vincent C. Pigott and Eugenia W. Herbert, 1–23. London: Routledge.
Krajick, Kevin
2005   Fire in the Hole: Raging in Mines from Pennsylvania to China, Coal Fires Threaten Towns, Poison Air and Water, and Add to Global Warming. *Smithsonian Magazine* 36, no. 2 (May): 52–61.
Kulikoff, Allan
1992   *The Agrarian Origins of American Capitalism*. Charlottesville: University Press of Virginia.
1989   The Transition to Capitalism in Rural America. *William and Mary Quarterly* 46 (January): 120–144.

Kumar, Pradeep

1992 *A Structural Analysis of Patented Bollman Suspension Trusses.* Morgantown, W.Va.: Institute for the History of Technology and Industrial Archaeology.

Lamoreaux, Naomi R.

1994 *Insider Lending, Banks, Personal Connections, and Economic Development in Industrial New England.* New York: Cambridge University Press.

Larcom, Lucy

1970 [1875] *An Idyl of Work.* Westport, Conn.: Greenwood Press.

1890 *A New England Girlhood: Outline from Memory.* Boston: Houghton Mifflin.

Larsen, Eric

1994 A Boardinghouse Madonna—Beyond the Aesthetics of a Portrait Created Through Medicine Bottles. In *An Archaeology of Harpers Ferry's Commercial and Residential District*, edited by Paul A. Shackel and Susan E. Winter. *Historical Archaeology* 28 (4): 68–79.

Laurie, Bruce

1989 *Artisans into Workers: Labor in 19th Century America.* New York: Hill and Wang.

Leary, Thomas E.

1979 Industrial Archaeology and Industrial Ecology. *Radical History Review* 21:171–182.

Leff, Mark H.

1995 Revisioning United States Political History. *American Historical Review* 100:833.

Leone, Mark P.

1995 A Historical Archaeology of Capitalism. *American Anthropologist* 97 (2): 251–268.

1988 The Georgian Order as the Order of Merchant Capitalism in Annapolis, Maryland. In *The Recovery of Meaning: Historical Archaeology in the Eastern United States*, edited by Mark P. Leone and Parker B. Potter Jr., 235–261. Washington, D.C.: Smithsonian Institution Press.

1984 Interpreting Ideology in Historical Archaeology: Using the Rules of Perspective in the William Paca Garden, Annapolis, Maryland. In *Ideology, Power, and Prehistory*, edited by Daniel Miller and Christopher Tilley, 25–35. Cambridge: Cambridge University Press.

Leone, Mark P., and Barbara J. Little

1993 Artifacts as Expressions of Society and Culture: Subversive Genealogy and the Value of History. In *History from Things: Essays on Material Culture*, edited by Stephen Lubar and W. David Kingery, 160–181. Washington, D.C.: Smithsonian Institution Press.

Leone, Mark P., and Parker B. Potter

1999 *Historical Archaeologies of Capitalism.* New York: Plenum.

Levin, Jed

1985 Drinking on the Job: How Effective was Capitalist Work Discipline? *American Archaeology* 5 (3): 195–201.

Lewis, Kenneth E.
1984 *The American Frontier: An Archaeological Study of Settlement Pattern and Process.*
New York: Academic Press.

Lewis, Mary E.
2002 Impact of Industrialization: Comparative Study of Child Health in Four Sites
from Medieval and Postmedieval England (A.D. 850–1859). *American Journal of
Physical Anthropology* 119 (3): 211–223.

Lewis, Ronald L.
1979 *Coal, Iron, and Slaves: Industrial Slavery in Maryland and Virginia.* Westport,
Conn.: Greenwood Press.

Libby, Jean
1991 African Ironmaking Culture Among African American Ironworkers in Western
Maryland, 1760–1850. Master's thesis, Ethnic Studies, San Francisco State University, San Francisco.

Lightfoot, Kent G.
1995 Culture Contact Studies: Redefining the Relationship between Prehistoric and
Historical Archaeology. *American Antiquity* 60 (2): 199–217.

Lightfoot, Kent G., Thomas A. Wake, and Ann M. Schiff
1993 Native Responses to the Russian Mercantile Colony of Fort Ross, California. *Journal of Field Archaeology* 20:159–175.

Linebaugh, Donald W.
2005 *The Man Who Found Thoreau: Roland W. Robbins and the Rise of Historical Archaeology in America.* Hanover, N.H.: University Press of New England.

2000 Forging a Career: Roland W. Robbins and Iron Industry Sites in the Northeastern
U.S. *IA: Journal of the Society for Industrial Archaeology* 26 (1): 11–18.

Lingenfelter, Richard
1974 *The Hardrock Miners: A History of the Mining Labor Movement in the American
West, 1863–1893.* Berkeley and Los Angeles: University of California Press.

Little, Barbara J.
1997 Expressing Ideology without a Voice, or, Obfuscation and the Enlightenment.
International Journal of Historical Archaeology 1 (3): 223–241.

1994 People with History: An Update on Historical Archaeology in the United States.
Journal of Archaeological Method and Theory 1 (1): 5–40.

Little, Barbara J., and Nancy J. Kassner
2001 Archaeology in the Alleys of Washington, DC. In *The Archaeology of Urban Landscapes: Explorations in Slumland,* edited by Alan Mayne and Tim Murry, 57–68.
New York: Cambridge University Press.

Lowenthal, David
1996 *Possessed by the Past: The Heritage Crusade and the Spoils of History.* New York:
Free Press.

1985 *The Past Is a Foreign Country.* New York: Cambridge University Press.

Lucas, Michael T.
1994 An Armory Worker's Life: Glimpses of Industrial Life. In *An Archeology of an
Armory Worker's Household: Park Building 48, Harpers Ferry National Historical*

Park, edited by Paul A. Shackel, 5.1–5.40. Occasional Report No. 12. Washington, D.C.: U.S. Department of the Interior, National Park Service.

Lucas, Michael, and Paul A. Shackel

1994 Changing Social and Material Routine in 19th-Century Harpers Ferry. In *An Archaeology of Harpers Ferry's Commercial and Residential District*, edited by Paul A. Shackel and Susan E. Winter. *Historical Archaeology* 28 (4): 27–36.

Ludlow Collective

2001 Archaeology of the Colorado Coal Field War, 1913–1914. In *Archaeologies of the Contemporary Past*, edited by Victor Buchli and Gavin Lucas, 94–107. London: Routledge Press.

Martin, Edgar W.

1942 *The Standard of Living in 1860: American Consumption Levels on the Eve of the Civil War*. Chicago: University of Chicago Press.

Marx, Leo

1964 *The Machine in the Garden: Technology and the Pastoral Ideal in America*. New York: Oxford University Press.

Mayne, Alan, and Tim Murry

2001 The Archeology of Urban Landscapes: Explorations in Slumland. In *The Archaeology of Urban Landscapes: Explorations in Slumland*, edited by Alan Mayne and Tim Murry, 1–7. New York: Cambridge University Press.

Mayne, Alan, and Tim Murry, eds.

2001 *The Archaeology of Urban Landscapes: Explorations in Slumland*. New York: Cambridge University Press.

McConnell, Stuart

1992 *Glorious Contentment: The Grand Army of the Republic, 1865–1900*. Chapel Hill: University of North Carolina Press.

McCracken, Grant

1988 *Culture and Consumption: New Approaches to the Symbolic Character of Goods and Activities*. Bloomington: Indiana University Press.

McGuire, Randall H.

2002 *A Marxist Archaeology*. Clinton Corners, N.Y.: Percheron Press.

1991 Building Power in the Cultural Landscape of Broome County, New York, 1880 to 1940. In *The Archaeology of Inequality*, edited by Randall H. McGuire and Robert Paynter, 102–124. Cambridge, Mass.: Blackwell.

1988 Dialogues with the Dead: Ideology and the Cemetery. In *The Recovery of Meaning: Historical Archaeology in the Eastern United States*, edited by Mark P. Leone and Parker B. Potter Jr., 435–480. Washington, D.C.: Smithsonian Institution Press.

McGuire, Randall H., and Paul Reckner

2002 The Unromantic West: Labor, Capital and Struggle. *Historical Archaeology* 36 (3): 44–58.

McKendrick, Neil, John Brewer, and J. H. Plumb

1982 *The Birth of a Consumer Society: The Commercialization of Eighteenth-Century England*. Bloomington: Indiana University Press.

Merrill, Michael
1995 Putting Capitalism in Its Place: A Review of Recent Literature. *William and Mary Quarterly* 52 (April): 315–326.

Metheny, Karen Bescherer
2007 *From the Miners' Doublehouse: Archaeology and Landscape in a Pennsylvania Coal Company Town*. Knoxville: University of Tennessee Press.

Militant
2005 Utah Miners' Union Fight Prominent at Colorado Event: Ten UMWA District 22 Locals at Ludlow Massacre Commemoration. *Militant* 69, no. 24 (June 27), http://www.themilitant.com/2005/6924/index.shtml (accessed December 28, 2005).

Miller, Carol Poh
2003 Study Tour Takes a Close-up Look at Sweden's Industrial Heritage. *Society for Industrial Archaeology Newsletter* 31 (1): 1–8, 17.

Miller, Daniel
1995 Consumption Studies as the Transformation of Anthropology. In *Acknowledging Consumption: A Review of New Studies*, edited by Daniel Miller, 264–295. London: Routledge.
1987 *Material Culture as Mass Consumption*. New York: Blackwell.

Miller, Daniel, and Christopher Tilley
1984 Ideology, Power and Prehistory: An Introduction. In *Ideology, Power and Prehistory*, edited by Daniel Miller and Christopher Tilley, 1–12. New York: Cambridge University Press.

Miller, George L.
1991 A Revised Set of CC Index Values for Classification and Economic Scaling of English Ceramics from 1787 to 1880. *Historical Archaeology* 25 (1): 1–25.
1980 Classification and Economic Scaling of 19th-Century Ceramics. *Historical Archaeology* 14:1–40.

Miller, George L., and Robert Hunter Jr.
1990 English Shell Edged Earthenware: Alias Leeds Ware, Alias Feather Edge. *Proceedings of the 35th Annual Wedgwood International Seminar*, 107–136.

Miller, George L., Ann Smart Martin, and Nancy Dickinson
1994 Changing Consumption Patterns: English Ceramics and the American Marker from 1770–1840. In *Everyday Life in the Early Republic:1789–1828*, edited by Catherine E. Hutching, 219–246. Winterthur, Del.: Henry Francis du Pont Winterthur Museum.

Miller, Randall
1981 The Fabric of Control: Slavery in Antebellum Southern Textile Mills. *Business History Review* 55 (4): 471–490.

Mills, Peter R., and Antoinette Martinez
1997 *The Archaeology of Russian Colonialism in North and Tropical Pacific*. Kroeber Anthropological Society Papers, Number 81. University of California, Berkeley.

Minchinton, Walter
1983 World Industrial Archaeology: A Survey. *World Archaeology* 15 (2): 125–136.

Money-Making for Ladies
1882   *Harper's New Monthly Magazine* 65, no. 385 (June): 112–116.

Montgomery, David
1979   *Worker's Control in America: Studies in the History of Work, Technology, and Labor Struggle.* New York: Cambridge University Press.

Mosher, Anne E.
1995   "Something Better than the Best": Industrial Restructuring, George McMurtry and the Creation of the Model Industrial Town of Vandergrift, Pennsylvania, 1883–1901. *Annals of the Association of American Geographers* 85 (1): 84–107.

Mrozowski, Stephen A.
2006   *The Archaeology of Class in Urban America.* New York: Cambridge University Press.
2000   The Growth of Managerial Capitalism and the Subtleties of Class Analysis in Historical Archaeology. In *Lines that Divide: Historical Archaeologies of Race, Class, and Gender,* edited by James A. Delle, Stephen A. Mrozowski, and Robert Paynter, 276–305. Knoxville: University of Tennessee Press.

Mrozowski, Stephen A., Grace H. Zeising, and Mary C. Beaudry
1996   *Living on the Boott: Historical Archeology at the Boott Mills Boardinghouses, Lowell, Massachusetts.* Amherst: University of Massachusetts Press.

Mukerji, Chandra
1983   *From Graven Images: Patterns of Modern Materialism.* New York: Columbia University Press.

Mullins, Paul R.
1996   Negotiating Industrial Capitalism: Mechanisms of Change among Agrarian Potters. In *Historical Archaeology: The Study of American Culture,* edited by Lu Ann DeCunzo and Bernard L. Herman, 151–191. Knoxville: Henry Francis Du Pont Winterthur Museum, University of Tennessee Press.

Murry, R. E.
1998   *The Lexicon of Labor.* New York: New Press.

Murshed, Madiha
2001   Unraveling Child Labor and Labor Legislation. *Journal of International Affairs* 40:173–174.

Nassaney, Michael S., and Marjorie R. Abel
2000   Urban Spaces, Labor Organization, and Social Control: Lessons from New England's Nineteenth-Century Cutlery Industry. In *Lines that Divide: Historical Archaeologies of Race, Class, and Gender,* edited by James A. Delle, Stephen A. Mrozowski, and Robert Paynter, 239–275. Knoxville: University of Tennessee Press.
1993   The Political and Social Contexts of Cutlery Production in the Connecticut Valley. *Dialectical Anthropology* 18:247–289.

Nassaney, Michael S, Alan H. McArdle, and Peter Stott
1989   Archaeological Locational Site Evaluation, and Data Recovery at the Russell-Harrington Cutlery Site, Turner Falls, Massachusetts. Amherst: UMass Archaeological Services, University of Massachusetts.

National Park Service (NPS)

1983   *Hopewell Furnace: A Guide to Hopewell Village National Historic Site.* Washington, D.C.: Department of the Interior.

Nevell, Michael

2005   The Social Archaeology of Industrialization: The Example of Manchester during the 17th and 18th Centuries. In *Industrial Archaeology: Future Directions*, edited by Eleanor C. Casella and James Symonds, 177–204. New York: Springer.

Noël Hume, Ivor

1983   *Here Lies Virginia: An Archaeologist's View of Colonial Life and History.* New York: Knopf.

Nottingham Castle Museum

1988   *Ruins in British Romantic Art from Wilson to Turner.* Nottingham, UK: Nottingham Castle Museum Nottingham.

Ollman, Bertell

1993   *Dialectical Investigations.* New York: Routledge.

Orser, Charles E., Jr.

2007   *The Archaeology of Race and Racialization in Historic America.* Gainesville: University Press of Florida.

1996   *A Historical Archaeology of the Modern World.* New York: Plenum.

1994   Toward a Global Historical Archaeology: An Example from Brazil. *Historical Archaeology* 28 (1): 5–22.

1988   The Archaeological Analysis of Plantation Society: Replacing Status and Caste with Economics and Power. *American Antiquity* 53 (4): 735–751.

Palmer, Marilyn

2005   Industrial Archaeology: Constructing a Framework of Inference. In *Industrial Archaeology: Future Directions*, edited by Eleanor C. Casella and James Symonds, 59–75. New York: Springer.

1990   Industrial Archaeology: A Thematic or a Period Discipline? *Antiquity* 64 (243): 275–282.

Palmer, Marilyn, and Peter Neaverson

1998   *Industrial Archaeology: Principles and Practice.* New York: Routledge.

Palus, Matthew, and Paul A. Shackel

2006   *"They Worked Regular": Craft, Labor, Family and the Archaeology of an Industrial Community.* Knoxville: University of Tennessee Press.

Pappas, Efstathios

2004   Fictive Kin in the Mountains: The Paternalistic Metaphor and Households in a California Logging Camp. In *Household Chores and Household Choices: Theorizing the Domestic Sphere in Historical Archaeology*, edited by Kerri S. Barile and Jamie C. Brandon, 159–176. Tuscaloosa: University of Alabama Press.

Parloa, Maria

1893   Division of the Family Income, Part 2. *Ladies' Home Journal* 10 (3): 19.

Paynter, Robert

2000a Historical and Anthropological Archaeology: Forging Alliances. *Journal of Archaeological Research* 8 (1): 1–37.

2000b Historical Archaeology and the Post-Columbian World of North America. *Journal of Archaeological Research* 8 (3): 169–217.

1989 The Archaeology of Equality and Inequality. *Annual Review of Anthropology* 18:369–99.

1988 Steps to an Archaeology of Capitalism. In *The Recovery of Meaning: Historical Archaeology in the Eastern United States,* edited by Mark P. Leone and Parker B. Potter Jr., 407–433. Washington, D.C.: Smithsonian Institution Press.

1985 Surplus Flow between Frontiers and Homelands. In *The Archaeology of Frontiers and Boundaries,* edited by Stanton W. Green and Stephen M. Perlman, 163–211. Orlando, Fla.: Academic Press.

1982 *Models of Spatial Inequality: Settlement Patterns in Historical Archaeology.* New York: Academic Press.

Paynter, Robert, and Randall H. McGuire

1991 The Archaeology of Inequality: Material Culture, Domination and Resistance. In *The Archaeology of Inequality,* edited by Randall McGuire and Robert Paynter, 1–27. Cambridge, Mass.: Basil Blackwell.

Pletka, Karyn L.

1993 Industrial Archaeology at the Robinson-Herring Sawmill Site, Greenbush, Wisconsin. *Michigan Archaeologist* 39 (1): 1–35.

Powell, Colin

2002 Special Briefing on Release of Trafficking in Persons Report, June 2002. U.S. Department of the State, Washington, D.C. http://www.state.gov/secretary/former/powell/remarks/2002/10748.htm/ (accessed March 23, 2008).

Praetzellis, Adrian, Mary Praetzellis, and Marley Brown III

1987 Artifacts as Symbols of Identity: An Example from Sacramento's Gold Rush Era Chinese Community. In *Living in Cities: Current Research in Urban Archaeology,* edited by Edward Staski, 38–47. Society for Historical Archaeology Special Publication Series, 5.

Praetzellis, Mary, and Adrian Praetzellis

1990 *Junk! Archaeology of the Pioneer Junk Store, 1877–1908.* Paper in Northern California Anthropology 4. Anthropology Studies Center, Sonoma State University, Rohnert Park, Calif.

Prude, Jonathan

1983 *The Coming of Industrial Order: Town and Factory Life in Rural Massachusetts, 1810–1860.* New York: Cambridge University Press.

Quinn, David Beers

1985 *Set Fair for Roanoke: Voyages and Colonies, 1584–1606.* Chapel Hill: University of North Carolina Press.

Reinhard, Karl J.
1994   Sanitation and Parasitism of Postbellum Harpers Ferry. In *An Archaeology of Harpers Ferry's Commercial and Residential District*, edited by Paul A. Shackel and Susan E. Winter. *Historical Archaeology* 28 (4): 63–67.

Reinhard, Karl J., Stephen A. Mrozowski, and Kathleen A. Orloski
1986   Privies, Pollen, Parasites and Seeds: A Biological Nexus in Historical Archaeology. *MASCA Journal* 4 (1): 31–36.

Riis, Jacob
1970   *How the Other Half Lives: Studies Among the Tenements of New York*. Cambridge: Harvard University Press.

Robinson, Harriet H.
1976 [1898]   *Looms and Spindles or Life Among the Early Mill Girls*. Kailua, Hawaii: Press Pacifica.

Rogers, R. Vashon, Jr.
1884   *The Law of Hotel Life, or the Wrongs and Rights of Host and Guest*. San Francisco: Sumner Whitney.

Rorer, S. T.
1899   The Boarding-House Table. *Ladies' Home Journal* 16 (12): 29.

Ross, Steven J.
1985   *Workers on the Edge: Work, Leisure, and Politics in Industrializing Cincinnati, 1788–1890*. New York: Columbia University Press.

Roth, Michael
1997   Irresistible Decay: Ruins Reclaimed. In *Irresistible Decay*, edited by Michael Roth, Claire Lyons and Charles Merewether, 1–23. Los Angeles: Getty Research Institute for the History of the Arts and Humanities.

Rovner, Irwin
1994   Floral History by the Back Door: A Test of Phytolith Analysis in a Residential Yard at Harpers Ferry. In *An Archaeology of Harpers Ferry's Commercial and Residential District*, edited by Paul A. Shackel and Susan E. Winter. *Historical Archaeology* 28 (4): 37–48.

Ryan, Loretta A.
1989   The Remaking of Lowell and Its Histories: 1965–83. In *The Popular Perception of Industrial History*, edited by Robert Wible and Francis R. Walsh, 79–97. Lanham, Md.: American Association for State and Local History Library, University Publishing Associates.

Rynne, Colin
2006   *Ireland 1750–1930: An Archaeology*. Cork, Ireland: Collins Press.

Saitta, Dean J.
2007   *The Archaeology of Collective Action*. Gainesville: University Press of Florida.

Salyer, Lucy E.
1995   *Laws Harsh as Tigers; Chinese Immigrants and the Shaping of Modern Immigration Law*. Chapel Hill: University of North Carolina Press.

Saunders

1999   Sweatshops Aren't History: Museum Traces Resurgence of Sweatshops in Exhibit Apparel Industry Tried to Stop. *New York Teacher*. Electronic document, http://www.newyorkteacher.org/ (accessed July 6, 2005).

Savulis, Ellen Rose

1992   Alternative Visions and Landscapes: Archaeology of the Shaker Social Order. In *Text-Aided Archaeology*, edited by Barbara J. Little, 195–203. Boca Raton, Fla.: CRC Press.

Schivelbusch, Wolfgang

1986   *The Railway Journey: The Industrialization of Time and Space in the Nineteenth Century*. Berkeley and Los Angeles: University of California Press.

Schlüter, Hermann

1910   *The Brewing Industry and the Brewery Workers' Movement in America*. Cincinnati: International Union of United Brewery Workmen of America.

Schmidt, Peter R.

1996   *Culture and Technology of African Iron Production*. Gainesville: University Press of Florida.

Schuyler, Robert L., and Christopher Mills

1976   The Supply Mill on Content Brook in Massachusetts. *Journal of Field Archaeology* 3:61–95.

Scott, James

1990   *Hidden Transcripts: Domination and the Arts of Resistance*. New Haven, Conn.: Yale University Press.

1985   *Weapons of the Weak: Everyday Forms of Peasant Resistance*. New Haven, Conn.: Yale University Press.

Sellars, Richard

1987   Vigil of Silence: The Civil War Memorials. *Courier*, March, 18–19.

Shackel, Paul A.

2004   Labor's Heritage: Remembering the American Industrial Landscape. *Historical Archaeology* 38:44–58.

2003   *Memory in Black and White: Race, Commemoration, and the Post-Bellum Landscape*. Walnut Creek, Calif.: AltaMira Press.

2001   Public Memory and the Search for Power in American Historical Archaeology. *American Anthropologist* 102 (3): 1–16.

2000a   *Archaeology and Created Memory: Public History in a National Park*. New York: Kluwer Academic/Plenum.

2000b   Craft to Wage Labor: Agency and Resistance in American Historical Archaeology. In *Agency Theory in Archaeology*, edited by John Robb and Marcia-Anne Dobres, 232–246. London: Routledge Press.

1999a   Public Memory and the Rebuilding the Nineteenth-Century Industrial Landscape at Harpers Ferry. *Quarterly Bulletin: Archeological Society of Virginia* 54 (3): 138–144.

1999b Town Planning and Nineteenth-Century Industrial Life in Harpers Ferry. In *The Archaeology of 19th-century Virginia*, edited by Theodore R. Reinhart and John H. Sprinkle Jr., 341–364. Council of Virginia Archaeologists, Special Publication No. 36 of the Archeological Society of Virginia.

1998 Classical and Liberal Republicanism and the New Consumer Culture. *International Journal of Historical Archaeology* 2 (1): 1–20.

1996 *Culture Change and the New Technology: An Archaeology of the Early American Industrial Era*. New York: Plenum.

1994 Memorializing Landscapes and the Civil War in Harpers Ferry. In *Look to the Earth: An Archaeology of the Civil War*, edited by Clarence Geier and Susan Winter, 256–270. Knoxville: University of Tennessee Press.

1993 *Personal Discipline and Material Culture: An Archaeology of Annapolis, Maryland, 1695–1870*. Knoxville: University of Tennessee Press.

Shackel, Paul A., and David A. Gadsby

2008 "I Wish for Paradise": Memory and Class in Hampden, Baltimore. In *Collaboration in Archaeological Practice: Engaging Descendant Communities*, edited by Chip Colwell-Chanthaphohn and T. J. Ferguson, 225–242. Lanham, Md.: AltaMira Press.

Shackel, Paul A., and David L. Larsen

2000 Labor, Racism, and the Built Environment in Early Industrial Harpers Ferry. In *Lines that Divide: Historical Archaeologies of Race, Class, and Gender*, edited by James Delle, Robert Paynter, and Stephen Mrozowski, 22–39. Knoxville: University of Tennessee Press.

Shackel, Paul A., and Matthew Palus

2006 The Gilded Age: An Archaeology of Working Class Communities. *American Anthropologist* 108 (4): 828–841.

Shanks, Michael, and Randall H. McGuire

1996 The Craft of Archaeology. *American Antiquity* 61: 75–88.

Shanks, Michael, and Christopher Tilley

1992 *ReConstructing Archaeology: Theory and Practice*, 2nd ed. New Studies in Archaeology. London: Routledge.

Sharp, Myron B., and William H. Thomas

1966 *A Guide to the Old Stone Blast Furnaces in Western Pennsylvania*. Pittsburgh: Historical Society of Western Pennsylvania.

Shelton, Cynthia

1986 *The Mills of Manayunk: Industrialization and Social Conflict in the Philadelphia Region, 1787–1837*. Baltimore: Johns Hopkins University Press.

Shephard, Steven J.

1987 Status Variation in Antebellum Alexandria: An Archaeological Study of Ceramic Tableware. In *Consumer Choice in Historical Archaeology*, edited by S. Spencer-Wood, 163–198. New York: Plenum.

Sheridan, Thomas E.

1998   Silver Shackles and Copper Collars: Race, Class and Labor in the Arizona Mining Industry from the Eighteenth Century until World War II. In *Social Approaches to an Industrial Past*, edited by A. Bernard Knapp, Vincent C. Pigott, and Eugenia W. Herbert, 174–187. New York: Routledge.

Silliman, Stephen W.

2006   Struggling with Labor, Working with Identities. In *Historical Archaeology*, edited by Martin Hall and Stephen W. Silliman, 147–166. Malden, Mass.: Blackwell.

2004   *Lost Laborers in Colonial California: Native Americans and the Archaeology of Rancho Petaluma*. Tucson: University of Arizona Press.

2001   Theoretical Perspectives on labor and Colonialism: Reconsidering the California Missions. *Journal of Anthropological Archaeology* 20 (4): 379–407.

Smith, Merritt Roe

1991   Industry, Technology, and the "Labor Question" in 19th-Century America: Seeking Synthesis. *Technology and Culture* 32 (3): 555–570.

1977   *Harpers Ferry Armory and the New Technology: The Challenge of Change*. Ithaca, N.Y.: Cornell University Press.

Solury, Theresa E.

1999   The Labor History Theme Study—Archaeology Component. Draft version. Manuscript on file, National Register of Historic Places, National Park Service, Washington, D.C.

South, Stanley

1988   Santa Elena: Threshold of Conquest. In *The Recovery of Meaning: Historical Archaeology in the Eastern United States*, edited by Mark P. Leone and Parker B. Potter Jr. 27–72. Washington, D.C.: Smithsonian Institution Press.

The Spirit of Discontent

1841   *Lowell Offering* 1:111–114.

Stansell, Christine

1987   *City of Women: Sex and Class in New York, 1789-1860*. New York: Knopf.

Starbuck, David

1986   The Shaker Mills in Canterbury, New Hampshire. *Industrial Archaeology* 12 (1): 11–38.

1984   The Shaker Concept of Household. *Man in the Northeast* 28:73–86.

Starobin, Robert S.

1970   *Industrial Slavery in the Old South*. New York: Oxford University Press.

Stocking, George W., Jr.

1985   Philanthropoids and Vanishing Cultures: Rockefeller Funding and the End of the Museum Era in Anglo-American Anthropology. In *Objects and Others: Essays on Museums and Material Culture*, vol. 3, edited by George W. Stocking Jr., 112–145. History of Anthropology series. Madison: University of Wisconsin Press.

1982   The Santa Fe Style in American Anthropology: Regional Interest, Academic Initiative, and Philanthropic Policy in the First Two Decades of the Laboratory of Anthropology, Inc. *Journal of the History of the Behavioral Sciences* 18:3–19.

1981 Anthropological Visions and Economic Realities in the 1930s Southwest. *El Palacio: Magazine of the Museum of New Mexico* 87 (3): 14–17.

Strasser, Susan

1982 *Never Done: A History of American Housework*. New York: Pantheon Books.

Stratton, Michael, and Barrie Trinder

2000 *Twentieth Century Industrial Archaeology*. London: E&FN Spon.

Striker, Michael, and Roderick Sprague

1993 Excavations at the Warren Chinese Mining Camp Site, 1989–1992. Report to the Forest Supervisor's Office, Payette National Forest, McCall, Idaho.

Sunstein, Cass R.

2004 We Need to Reclaim the Second Bill of Rights. *Chronicle of Higher Education*, June 11, B9–B10.

Taksa, Lucy

2005 The Material Culture of an Industrial Artifact: Interpreting Control, Defiance, and Everyday Resistance at the New South Wales Eveleigh Railway Workshop. *Historical Archaeology* 39 (3): 8–27.

Taylor, George R.

1951 *The Transportation Revolution, 1815–1836*. New York: Rinehart.

Teague, George

1987 The Archaeology of Industry in North America. Ph.D. diss., Department of Anthropology, University of Arizona.

Thomas, David H., ed.

1991 *Columbian Consequences*. Vol. 3, *The Spanish Borderlands in Pan-American Perspective*. Washington, D.C.: Smithsonian Institution Press.

1990 *Columbian Consequences*. Vol. 2, *Archaeological and Historical Perspectives on the Spanish Borderlands East*. Washington, D.C.: Smithsonian Institution Press.

1989 *Columbian Consequences*. Vol. 1, *Archaeological and Historical Perspectives on the Spanish Borderlands West*. Washington, D.C.: Smithsonian Institution Press.

Thompson, E. P.

1967 Time, Work-Discipline and Industrial Capitalism. *Past and Present* 38:56–97.

1966 *The Making of the English Working Class*. New York: Vintage Books.

Tilley, Christopher

1990 Michel Foucault: Towards an Archaeology of Archaeology. In *Reading Material Culture*, edited by Christopher Tilley, 281–347. London: Blackwell.

Tomaso, Matthew S., Richard F. Veit, Carissa A. De Rooy, and Stanley L. Walling

2006 Social Status and Landscape in a Nineteenth-Century Planned Industrial Alternative Community: Archaeology and Geography of Feltville, New Jersey. *Historical Archaeology* 40 (1): 20–36.

Trinder, Barrie

1983 New Course in Industrial Archaeology. *World Archaeology* 15 (2): 218–223.

Trinder, B., and N. Cox, eds.

2000 *Miners and Mariners of the Severn Gorge: Probate Inventories for Benthall, Broseley, Little Wenlock and Madeley, 1660–1764*. Chichester, W. Sussex, UK: Phillimore.

Tunick, Susan

1986   *Field Guide to Apartment Building Architecture: An Illustrated Overview Providing a Simple Way to Identify Building Parts, Styles and Materials.* New York State: Friend of Terra Cotta.

Twain, Mark, and Charles Dudley Warner

1972 [1873]   *The Gilded Age: A Tale of To-Day.* Indianapolis: Bobbs-Merrill.

UNESCO

2007   Industrial Heritage. United Nations Educational, Scientific Cultural Organization (UNESCO). Electronic document, http://whc.unesco.org/sites/industrial. htm/ (accessed July 18, 2007).

University of Denver Magazine

2003   The Work of a DU Archaeologist Is Illuminating One of the Darkest Episodes in the History of U.S. Organized Labor. *Denver Magazine*, Winter. Electronic document, http://www.du.edu/dumagazine/winter2003/feature_ludlow.html/ (accessed March 1, 2008).

Urry, John

1990   *The Tourist Gaze: Leisure and Travel in Contemporary Societies.* London: Sage.

Van Bueren, Thad M., ed.

2002   Communities Defined by Work: Life in Western Work Camps. *Historical Archaeology* 36 (3).

Van der Bent, Teunis J.

1917   *The Planning of Apartment Houses, tenements, and Country Homes. A Text Book for Students of Architecture, Household Arts, Practical Arts and Hygiene of Private and Institutional Dwellings; A Guide for Architects, Superintendents and Managers of Various Types of Institutions.* New York: Brentando's.

Vogel, Lise

1977   Hearts to Feel and Tongues to Speak: New England Mill Women in the Early Nineteenth Century. In *Class, Sex, and the Women Worker*, edited by Milton Cantor and Bruce Ware, 64–82. Westport, Conn.: Greenwood Press.

Voss, Barbara L.

2005   The Archaeology of Overseas Chinese Communities. *World Archaeology* 37 (3): 424–439.

Walker, Mark

2000   Labor History at the Ground Level: Colorado Coalfield War Archaeology Project. *Labor's Heritage* 11 (1): 58–75.

1999   Archaeology, Audience, and the Memory of Miners. Paper presented at the Society for Historical Archaeology Conference on Historical and Underwater Archeology, Salt Lake City, Utah.

Wall, Diana DiZerega

1994   *The Archaeology of Gender: Separating the Spheres in Urban America.* New York: Plenum.

Wallace, Anthony F. C.

1982   *St. Claire, a Pennsylvania Coal Mining Community*. New York: W. W. Norton.

1978   *Rockdale: The Growth of an American Village in the Early Industrial Revolution*. New York: Vintage Books.

Wallerstein, Immanuel

1989   *The Modern World System*. Vol. 3. San Diego: Academic Press.

1980   *The Modern World System*. Vol. 2 New York: Academic Press.

1976   *The Modern World System*. Vol. 1. New York: Academic Press.

Wegars, Priscilla

1991   Who's Been Workin' on the Railroad? An Examination of the Construction, Distribution, and Ethnic Origins of Domes Rock Ovens on Railroad Related Sites. *Historical Archaeology* 25 (2): 37–60.

Weir, Robert E., and James P. Hanlan, eds.

2004   *Historical Encyclopedia of American Labor*, Vol. 1, *A–O*. Westport, Conn.: Greenwood Press.

Weitzman, David L.

1980   *Traces of the Past: A Field Guide to Industrial Archaeology*. New York: Scribner.

Wesolowsky, Tony

1996   A Jewel in the Crown of Old King Coal: Eckley Miners' Village. *Pennsylvania Heritage Magazine* 22 (1). Electronic document, http://www.phmc.state.pa.us/ppet/eckley/ (accessed July 17, 2003).

Williams, David

2005   *A People's History of the Civil War: Struggles for the Meaning of Freedom*. New York: New Press.

Williams, Jack S.

1992   The Archaeology of Underdevelopment and the Military Frontier of Northern New Spain. *Historical Archaeology* 26 (1): 7–21.

Williams, John Hoyt

1985   Indiana's New Harmony. *Early American Life* 16 (2): 53–71.

Wolf, Eric

1982   *Europe and the People Without History*. Berkeley and Los Angeles: University of California Press.

Wood, Margaret

2004   Working Class Households as Sites of Social Change. In *Household Chores and Household Choices: Theorizing the Domestic Sphere in Historical Archaeology*, edited by Kerri S. Barile and Jamie C. Brandon, 159–176. Tuscaloosa: University of Alabama Press.

2002   *Fighting for Our Homes: An Archaeology of Women's Domestic Labor and Social Change in a Working Class, Coal Mining Community, 1900–1930*. Ph.D. diss., Department of Anthropology, Syracuse University.

Workman, Michael E., Paul Salstrom, and Philip W. Ross

1994   *Northern West Virginia Coal Fields: Historical Context*. Morgantown, W.Va.: Institute for the History of Technology and Industrial Archaeology.

Wurst, LouAnn, and Randall H. McGuire

1999 Immaculate Consumption: A Critique of the "Shop Till You Drop" School of Human Behavior. *International Journal of Historical Archaeology* 3 (3): 191–199.

Yamin, Rebecca

2002 Children's Strikes, Parents' Rights: Patterson and Five Points. *International Journal of Historical Archaeology* 6 (2): 113–126.

2000 Health and Hygiene in an Urban Context. In *Tales of Five Points: Working-Class Life in Nineteenth-Century New York*. Vol. 1, *A Narrative History and Archaeology of Block 160*, edited by Rebecca Yamin, 338–370. West Chester, Pa.: John Milner.

1998 Lurid Tales and Homely Stories of New York's Notorious Five Points. *Historical Archaeology* 32 (1): 74–85.

Yamin, Rebecca, ed.

2001 Becoming New York: The Five Points Neighborhood. *Historical Archaeology* 35 (3).

Zinn, Howard

2003 *Passionate Declarations: Essays on War and Justice*. New York: HarperCollins.

Zonderman, David A.

1992 *Aspirations and Anxieties: New England Workers and the Mechanized Factory System, 1815–1850*. New York: Oxford University Press.

Index

Paul A. Shackel is professor of anthropology at the University of Maryland and is director of the Center for Heritage Resource Studies. He is the author of several books, including *Myth, Memory, and the Making of the American Landscape* (2001) and coeditor of *Places in Mind: Public Archaeology as Applied Anthropology* (2004).